Marriage:
Top Priority

Jeanette + Elvis

By now you probably get the
hint that we like giving books
as gifts, It is encouraging to see
how God is beginning to bless your
family. Love + God Bless:

Diane, George +
Jonathan xxx

THE SHRIER FAMILY: Pastor and Mrs. John C. Shrier, with Paul, Kevin and Pamela.

Marriage: Top Priority

John C. Shrier
Foreword by Don Wilkerson

G.R. WELCH COMPANY, LIMITED
Burlington   **Ontario**

Scripture passages quoted in *Marriage: Top Priority* are from the King James
Version of The Holy Bible, unless indicated otherwise.

ISBN: 0-919532-57-8

©1980 G.R. Welch Company, Limited

G.R. Welch Company, Limited
960 Gateway
Burlington, Ontario
L7L 5K7   Canada

Printed in Canada

To
my beloved wife
Doris

"If American families are to survive the incredible stresses and dangers they now face, *it will be because husbands and fathers provide loving leadership in their homes,* placing their wives and children at the highest level on their system of priorities." *

Dr. James C. Dobson

* From *Straight Talk to Men and Their Wives* by Dr. James C. Dobson. (Waco, Texas: Word Books, 1980) Used with the permission of the publisher.

Contents

Foreword

John Shrier has written a practical, scriptural, and thorough book on marriage and its related needs, problems and challenges.

His opening chapter on marriage priority in relationship to church, ministry, job, and personal lifestyle, should be required reading for all active church members, deacons, pastors, and church staff. Pastor Shrier goes on from there to cover a wide spectrum of topics pertinent to a successful marriage and family life.

Marriage: Top Priority has an important and timely message for young couples; those in the "stretch run" of their married lives, and for about-to-be-married couples. Shrier does not only treat the sacredness of marriage between two persons but he also effectively deals with it within a much larger context; treating marriage and its relationship to total living, total loving, and total Christianity.

Don Wilkerson
Teen Challenge Inc.
Brooklyn, N.Y.

Preface

Messages on marriage seem to meet a major need in our society today and I have noticed that when sermons on this subject are made available the response is the very best.

This book is based on a series of sermons that were preached, but not in sequence, so the compilation may or may not possess specific continuity. However, in publishing Bible-centered facts on the issues of married life, I have sought to inspire a deeper dedication to the marriage vows.

A young married man, speaking of the sermon on sex recounted here, recently said to me, "If I had read that sermon five years ago I could have saved my marriage." I pray that some of these other messages will arrive "in time" to save many more.

There are all kinds of pressures that build up in the marriage relationship that can lead to a crackup if they are not relieved. I have tried to deal with some of these problems, and in doing so am reminded of one leader who listed them as follows: *meddling, deliberate childishness, boredom, frustration, disappointment, differences of religious convictions, jealousy, emotional-physical-intellectual immaturity,* and *nagging.*

My fervent desire is that this little book will come into the hands of those who seek an answer to all these plaguing problems. So many young people are blind to the simple facts, and some others have chosen to ignore them to their own hurt.

Over the span of my ministry I have become more and more convinced that *priority* principles are a powerful influence in our lives, and during a seventeen-year period of pastoring in the city of Waterloo, Ontario, I was able to see these priorities tested in the full flow of church life.

Leadership was governed by these principles, and they were proven under severe stress as our growing congregation expanded, outgrowing two sanctuaries and moving into a third building accommodating eleven hundred people. All this happened within a period of twelve years. This exceptional growth greatly increased the demands upon leadership, but still, the individual person, his or her marriage, and family relationships always took precedence.

During the appointment of elders to oversee the growing spiritual needs of the congregation, one man chosen responded by sharing a problem that would limit his service: 'My wife is not very well and the responsibility in management makes it impossible to serve effectively."

The response of his fellow elders was very positive. There was a unanimous decision to appoint him, and accept his limited contribution until he would be free to give his position in the church the attention it required. This meant accepting his absence from various church activities until his personal affairs could be improved.

It was indeed a decision involving our complete support of his personal life needs. Now, all is well and he is serving very effectively.

Personal priorities must be our prime concern as Christians. It's the only possible way to strengthen the lives of church members. We are the larger family of God, and this can only become obvious as a witness when each family unit gains support from the church.

My marriage and my family must, under all social and spiritual pressures, remain my number one priority before God. My pastoral ministry is no stronger than my family life.

After a morning worship service recently one congregational member reinforced the significance of this principle. He simply said, "Pastor, I've always enjoyed your ministry, but what really impresses me is your family."

My first and continued prayer is that this will always be true.

John C. Shrier

1

Personal Life Priorities

Cultural conflict, crises and confusion make it virtually impossible to establish any personal life priorities.

Charles Hammel spoke of "jumbled priorities," which is certainly an appropriate and definitive term. But let us attempt to define the term "priority." It's simply this: "acting on a matter because of God's prior claim on my life which has precedence over all other human agencies or demands."

In his pamphlet, *The Tyranny of the Urgent,* Mr. Hammel tells of a time in his life when a cotton mill manager said to him, "Your greatest danger is letting the urgent or immediate demands from outside sources crowd out what is important."

The problem of "jumbled priorities" is one we all face quite regularly. The housewife lets urgent daily demands completely crowd out her devotional life. The busy businessman lets urgent appeals of success or labor crowd out extra hours with his Lord, or with his family. With God's priority list established for us in the book of Ephesians, it's important that we understand how crucial this list is to a successful life. Most of our problems in life are a result of having our priorities badly confused, so let's discover for ourselves what is the will of God regarding life and time.

In Ephesians 5:16,17 we read, "Redeeming the time, because the days are evil. Wherefore be ye not unwise, but understanding what the will of the Lord *is*." What is the will of the Lord regarding personal life priorities? You may say, "I only have so much time," and ask, "How can it most wisely be spent to the glory of God, and for the good of my family, my wife, my church and society?" This is what God is concerned about and this, therefore, has to become our personal concern.

Your Spiritual Life

It is just as important to know how to live as it is to know how to make a living. That's why God wants to build a life that has a definite spiritual dimension. We must understand that God is interested in gaining entrance into our lives. Jesus said, "For what is man profited, if he shall gain the whole world, and lose his own soul? or what shall a man give in exchange for his soul?" (Matthew 16:26).

It's a matter of priorities. Jesus is saying, give attention to spiritual things, for ". . . life consisteth not in the abundance of the things which he possesseth" (Luke 12:15).

It's a matter of who or what has control of our lives. The call is toward life on a higher plane. "And be not drunk with wine, wherein is excess; but be filled with (under the control of) the (Holy) Spirit" (Ephesians 5:18). It requires a surrender to the Holy Spirit, and ultimately to be "born" again. We know that we cannot enter the kingdom except we be born again; life in the spiritual realm requires the miracle of a spiritual birth. (John 3:3-5).

A businessman, a top man in his field, while driving down the main street of our city, cried out, "O God, what's it all about?" He said, "I was so frustrated, I said it out loud." The next day God impressed me, knowing nothing of the cry from this man's soul, to go and speak with him about Jesus Christ. I talked with him about serving God, and about making a surrender of his life to Jesus Christ. By eleven o'clock that evening he was on his knees surrendering his life to Jesus Christ as Lord of his life. That's what God wants.

We are called to ". . . Walk in the Spirit, and ye shall not fulfil the lust of the flesh" (Galatians 5:16). God is concerned that we should submit to the Spirit, and in this submission we should be able to build Christian character. This answers the question, "Why walk in the Spirit?" Because it affects our whole lifestyle! We learn to love our neighbors as we would want them to love us, "For all the law is fulfilled in one word, *even* in this; Thou shalt love thy neighbour as thyself" (Galatians 5:14). We learn to treat others around us with respect, and we won't be found chewing people out as in the past. We are warned: "But if ye bite and devour one another, take heed that ye be not consumed one of another" (Galatians 5:15).

We will find that under the control of the Holy Spirit we will be able to cope with contrary spirits. God's Spirit in us helps us. Where formerly we would get angry, or become overpowered with certain bad tempers, or certain bad attitudes, now the Holy Spirit gives us new strength. "For the flesh lusteth against the Spirit, and the Spirit against the flesh: and these are contrary the one to the other: so that ye cannot do the things that ye would" (Galatians 5:17).

Under the control of the Spirit we are free from sin's power. That power over us is broken. Sins such as mentioned in Galatians, Chapter 5 and Verses 18 to 21; "But if ye be led of the Spirit, ye are not under the law. Now the works of the flesh are manifest, which are *these*: Adultery, fornication, uncleanness, lasciviousness, Idolatry, witchcraft, hatred, variance, emulations, wrath, strife, seditions, heresies, Envyings, murders, drunkenness, revellings, and such like: . . ." This includes the whole gammit of sin's power. In the strength of God's power and presence these forces are destroyed and we become fruitful Christians.

This is God's perfect plan for every man and woman.

The real problem is how do we walk in the Spirit? That is again a matter of priorities. God reveals the secret in plain terms. "Speaking to yourselves in psalms and hymns and spiritual songs, singing and making melody in your heart to the Lord; Giving thanks always for all things unto God and the Father in the name of our Lord Jesus Christ; Submitting yourselves one to another in the fear of God" (Ephesians 5:19-21). Take this in order and discover how to walk in the Spirit. "Speaking to yourselves in psalms and hymns and spiritual songs." Read scriptures, memorize verses for the purposes of meditation. Learn to let the word of God dominate you and your thought life. After you make that initial submission to Christ, and surrender to His will, then walk in submission to Christ, according to the Holy Word. Get the thoughts of God into your mind, and know what God would want to do with your life on a day-to-day basis.

Further, you are to develop an attitude of gratitude. Learn to give thanks to God in all things, no matter whether they're good or bad. Whether it's a good day or a bad day, rise in the morning and say, "Thank God for another day; thank God for my health; thank God for my job." Start in the morning thanking God. Thank Him for your food. And never stop thanking Him for all things, throughout the entire day.

I remember when my wife and I were involved in a bad car accident. My wife barely escaped serious injury, and possible death. The car was a total write-off. When we arrived at the church that Sunday morning, I had a message ready on the subject of "Joy," but I had never felt less of the joy of the Lord than on that occasion. My wife, in spite of that shocking experience, stood and testified. She said, "All I could think of when that car hit us was, this is the will of God concerning you. In all things give thanks." She had an attitude of gratitude.

Some people find it very difficult to learn to be under the direction of the Spirit on a day-to-day basis. This again, emphasizes the importance of getting scripture into your mind, so that you understand what God's thoughts are for your life, and in all life situations. When you submit yourself, sometimes in situations where you feel you should retaliate, you will find that the Lord will strengthen you.

Paul teaches, "Let the word of Christ dwell in you richly in all wisdom; teaching and admonishing one another in psalms and hymns and spiritual songs, singing with grace in your hearts to the Lord. And whatsoever ye do (when you get up in the morning to go to your job) in word or deed, *do* all in the name of the Lord Jesus, giving thanks to God and the Father by him" (Colossians 3:16,17). "And whatsoever ye do, do *it* heartily, as to the Lord . . ." (Colossians 3:23).

Your Marriage

God wants to build a marriage. "Wives, submit yourselves unto your own husbands, as unto the Lord. For the husband is the head of the wife, even as Christ is the head of the church: and he is the saviour of the body. Therefore as the church is subject unto Christ, so *let* the wives *be* to their own husbands in every thing" (Ephesians 5:22-24).

"Husbands, love your wives, even as Christ also loved the church, and gave himself for it" (Ephesians 5:25).

The obvious demand that is laid upon husband and wife here is that of mutual cooperation. First, let it be very clear that two people who maintain a close relationship with Jesus Christ, discover how practical it is to fulfill their individual role as husband or as wife. The appeal is directed to the men. God wants your wife to come before your job and your church. Love means for better or for worse. It means sharing in her daily struggles — caring for her needs ahead of your own. This is definitely God's divine order for your life. God says, "Husbands, love your wives, and be not bitter against them" (Colossians 3:19).

The importance of how you treat your wife and how you act toward her has something to do with whether your prayers are going to be answered or not, so your marriage is very important to God.

In the past, we considered that God's first concern for us would be that we should help the church, that we should be better Sunday School teachers, serve on more committees, and be greater used of God in the church. Do you know that many times while we've been serving the church all those extra hours, our own marriages have been disintegrating? The priority that God places here is not the church ahead of the marriage. "Likewise, ye husbands, dwell with *them* according to knowledge, giving honour unto the wife, as unto the weaker vessel, and as being heirs together of the grace of life; that your prayers be not hindered" (I Peter 3:7).

Let me illustrate. A minister of youth in a large church thought surely that God was pleased with what he was doing. He was working seven days a week, reaching a minimum of eighty hours, just burning himself out for the life of the church, and he thought this was proper in God's sight. However, while he carried out his duties as a minister, his wife was taking second, or maybe third place, and his family was suffering in a similar fashion. Then God showed him this revelation of truth on the matter of marriage.

His wife became very ill with an extremely high fever. At the time there was an important building committee meeting planned for the extension of the youth department, and he was obviously the key man. There were a number of men involved in these board meetings, including the senior minister and other busy people. But God showed him that his wife was more important than the church, than his job. Under grave circumstances this priority came to the surface. His wife's fever was dangerously high. He knew what to do. He phoned the senior minister, declared that it was impossible for him to leave his wife to attend that meeting. Where previously he would have considered that the meeting came first, now he knew God wanted him to take care of his wife. The senior minister understood, accepted his explanation, had the other men informed, and the meeting was cancelled. He gained some friends, did what was right for his wife, and God was pleased.

God is more concerned about your marriage than he is

about whether or not you spend extra hours in the church.

Wives too must understand their responsibilities. To submit means accepting a share of her man's life. It means standing by him as he makes decisions involving the family. Whether they are weak decisions or strong, good or bad, he will make them better when his wife stands by him. A wife should support her husband in times of personal need, even when it means sacrificing her personal desires, in order to assist him and strengthen him as father and head of the house. "Even as Sara obeyed Abraham, calling him lord: whose daughters ye are, as long as ye do well, and are not afraid with any amazement" (I Peter 3:6).

So, it's very clear that God's number two priority is your marriage. How can you expect to be effective in your society, in your church, in your job, if it's at the expense of a happy marriage? If your marriage is a failure then all other areas of your life are immediately affected.

Your Family

God wants to build a life. God wants to build a marriage. God wants to build a family.

We must understand that the family is the very heart and core of society itself. It is the substance of society. Let's go back to the priority list as God has outlined it: "Children, obey your parents in the Lord: for this is right. Honour thy father and mother; which is the first commandment with promise; That it may be well with thee, and thou mayest live long on the earth. And, ye fathers, provoke not your children to wrath: but bring them up in the nurture and admonition of the Lord" (Ephesians 6:1-4).

Someone has well said, "Home is the cradle of eternity. Home is meant to be the preliminary of heaven." Again, it's the substance of society. The family circle is to be the supreme conductor of Christianity; it's where we should learn tenderness, humbleness, courtesy, self-forgetfulness, faith and sympathy. Your children come ahead of your job, and come ahead of your church, in terms of priorities. Nevertheless, your job is still important and your church is important, but I must re-emphasize that according to God's order of things, the family is worth more than extra hours on the job, or holding an extra office in the church. Your children are *more* important. That does not mean that the others do not matter. It means simply that the other things must not rob you of legitimate time and attention required for building a strong family structure. The Bible makes it very clear that if a minister does not control his own house he should not be controlling or leading in the house of God. One great preacher was asked, if he had a chance to do things differently what would he change. He said only one thing: "I would spend more time with my children."

If your job or your church takes every extra moment you have, until you have to neglect the spiritual and moral welfare of your family, you have "jumbled priorities." Again, let me illustrate.

I received a phone call one morning from my good and beloved wife. She said, "I want to see you." I replied that I would be home at lunch time, and we could talk then.

"No. I want to see you now." The tone was one of finality. I understood that I was being paged, and I was to be available immediately.

I went home quickly and she directed me to take a seat. "You have time to counsel with everyone," she said, "but now you just sit down right there and be quiet until I'm finished."

Then she opened up on me with both barrels.

She said, "Do you realize how little time you are spending at home?" (That was before I discovered these priorities as God has ordered them.) "Do you realize how much time you have for me, or for the children, or for home?"

At that time I was heading a district youth program involving 145 churches, pastoring a growing church, writing literature for nationwide youth evangelism, conducting youth seminars and evangelistic thrusts across Canada.

Needless to say, my energy was burning out and I had no time for anyone but the services I was supposedly carrying out "for the Lord."

After a considerable period of time I looked back at her and said, "Do you know something? You're absolutely right."

Well, I discovered as God gave me grace, that I could make some changes. But it wasn't until God allowed me to share these great priority insights that I really found out how to control, or govern, or direct my life according to the will of God.

Pastor Jerry Cook, writing on *Love, Acceptance and Forgiveness,* relates his position on personal priorities:

We do not appeal to families to support the church and its programs. Instead, we structure the church and its programs to support the family. We believe the family unit is central in God's plan.

Now, it would not be very consistent of us to take the position I just stated and then have the leaders of the church sacrificing their own family life for the sake of the "work of the Lord." If a staff member comes to me with a family problem, I say, "What do you need? Do you need time away? Do you need to go walk on the beach awhile with your wife? What? Anything you need, we'll help." Then I send him home and tell him I don't want to see him back in his office until things are OK at home.

Not long ago an elder came to me and said his children were getting hard to control, his wife was edgy, and he was troubled about his family. I asked him how long he thought he needed and he said six months. I told him to take a year and get things under control. If things were OK before that, fine. But he had a year free from any duties. All the other elders prayed with him and blessed him. I'm glad to report he's making fine progress and will soon be able to function effectively in a position of leadership again.

My own family is extremely important to me and I take

Monday every week to be with them. I am never available for anything else on Mondays, I don't care what it is. If you come to my house and knock on the door on a Monday, I will not answer it. I don't answer my phone. Only my secretary can reach me at an unlisted number, and that only in the most extreme circumstances.

I also set aside certain evenings for my family. Nothing violates that. Pressures of church business are never allowed to intrude. I consider that an act of love not only to God and my family but to the congregation. You see, I would have no ministry left if my home were to go.

*It's not that we have just decided to emphasize the family throughout the life of the congregation. God did. We're simply trying to listen to Him.**

Many men in various vocations in life figure the most important thing on earth is to be a success, to be productive, or fruitful as they interpret it, regardless of who suffers. God once acknowledged Abraham saying, "For I know him, that he will command his children and his household after him. . ." (Genesis 18:19). And you don't command your household from the office, from an airplane, or from any other place outside the home. Noah gained important recognition for leading his entire family into the ark of God. He chose their eternal safety as the most important thing on his priority list. Children have needs. They need attention both emotionally and physically. They need understanding. They need someone to talk to. They need someone to listen. They need personal acceptance, to establish their own worth and value system. They need a feeling of personal value by having their views respected if not totally accepted. At the same time, children are also called upon to help maintain, and strengthen and stabilize the family unit. Obedience to parents is not optional. It's God's will and if a child is responsible for upsetting the peace, or the spiritual strength of the family, God will hold that child accountable.

---

*Love, Acceptance and Forgiveness by Jerry Cook with Stanley C. Baldwin, Copyright, 1979 by G/L Publications, Ventura, CA. 93003.

I add this for the sake of the children. Let us not fail in our understanding that God works through the family. The family is the substance of society — the substance of the church. It's the substance of eternity.

Your Job

I am not impressed with the fact that I am in full-time service for Christ and you are not. Every child of God who names the name of Christ is in full-time service. ". . . as the servants of Christ, doing the will of God from the heart; With good will doing service, as to the Lord, and not to men: Knowing that whatsoever good thing any man doeth, the same shall he receive of the Lord, whether *he be* bond or free. And, ye masters (or bosses, or foremen) do the same things unto them, forbearing threatening: knowing that your Master also is in heaven; neither is there respect of persons with him" (Ephesians 6:6-9). "And whatsoever ye do, do *it* heartily, as to the Lord, and not unto men" (Colossians 3:23).

You are in full-time service every day you enter your office or go on to that campus. You are serving the Lord Christ over those books in the classroom, in that managerial position, in that warehouse, or on that assembly line.

This business of full-time service is often misunderstood. My vocation is a pastor. Your vocation is probably very different. However, I will answer for how I have conducted myself in my position, and you will answer for how you conduct yourself in your work. We are all serving the Lord Christ. Our vocation or job in life is of utmost importance. It's where we're able to work out the true spirit of Christ in our own lives. Character is developed in the full stream of life. Therefore, work produces character.

The great Henry Drummond made it very plain when he said:

. . . an office is not a place for making money, it's a place

for making character. A workshop is not for making machinery alone, it's a place for making men. Not for turning wood, or for fitting engines. To God's eye it is the place for founding of character. It is a place for fitting in the virtues to one's life, for turning out honest, modest tempered, God fearing men. Integrity, thoroughness, honesty, accuracy, conscientiousness, faithfulness, patience. These unseen things which complete a soul are woven into it at work. Apart from work these things are not. He who would ripen and perfect the eternal element in his being will do so by attending to the spiritual uses of his daily task, or his daily work so turning three-quarters of every day into an everlasting means of grace.

God has so designed life. Your job is important and God wants you to succeed. He wants you to know that you're serving Him every day.

However, the job must not take precedence over your family or your wife. Beware of those extra hours, the over-time spent making extra dollars, with an eye for the big buck. Sure you can make it. You can make it and ride high. You can push the success ladder right to the sky.

Having done all of that in terms of dollars — in terms of position or material things — have you then gone home to a shattered love life? Have you gone home to a disenchanted spouse, or a home wherein you are no longer accepted but as a stranger or a guest? Have you gone home to find that your marriage no longer exists? The spirit is gone?

You thought it was important that you should make money and prosper. You wanted your wife to be proud of you. She doesn't want to be proud of you as much as she wants to know you. She wants to live with you, to share your life, and you must share hers. Otherwise, having done all to succeed, you've failed because you have not done the will of God. But let's not forget that wives are called upon to assist, make sacrifices, and make complimentary contributions to see to it that your job does become successful. Even so, the job cannot detract from the marriage because that's

God's priority for you.

So you see, it's not that one is more important, it's that they're all important. You must know when the time comes to choose between giving your wife her fair place in your life, and going on that extra trip or spending extra hours out on the golf course somewhere. When you have to choose, remember that God's priority really is for you to be home with your children. What is more important to you, the extra money or your children? There is no question. The money is of little importance at that point, for the child's trust is in you. The commitment that's been made to your child for the benefit of his future and character development must come first. When it comes to a matter of how much time is left over for the family, that's when you have to make your decisions.

Your Ministry

God wants to build a ministry. ". . . to make known the mystery of the gospel, For which I am an ambassador in bonds: that therein I may speak boldly, as I ought to speak" (Ephesians 6:19,20).

We are to be clothed with the armour of God, to carry out a ministry; to wrestle against principalities and powers. He wants us to stand on the gospel, to have our feet shod with the preparation of the gospel, and to go forth against the fiery darts of the wicked, quenching them with the sword of the Spirit, praying in prayers and supplications, persevering.

The church is God's vehicle for doing His work. Every man has an individual ministry given to him by God. That ministry in your church may be very different from mine but it is a ministry. Now, I know that my ministry gift is an evangelist, and I know that God has given me that gift, but if I allow the ministry of an evangelist to overshadow and detract from the fact that I have commitments as a pastor, I have spoiled God's plan for my life.

You too have to fill your role in the church. You have

specific areas where you are most effective. The church needs you, whether it is in the capacity of Sunday School teacher, deacon, usher, musician, or in some other way according to his will. But some people get overbalanced in the direction of the church, where the church becomes more important than their marriage, more important than their family, and sometimes more important than their job. There are people who think it's essential to be at meetings here, there and everywhere — getting blessed. While they're getting blessed their family is sitting at home being cursed with their absence.

There are men who spend as high as ten, fifteen or twenty hours a week serving on up to five committees. They think that's the will of God. They expect the wife to understand and that the children should understand.

Do you know what I've been doing since I understood this revelation of truth? I've been suggesting that some men give up offices, and cut down on meetings. I believe God will give us other men to help fill the positions that are left vacant. These men will then have the proper amount of time to spend with their children, with their wives, with their jobs, or whatever the case and place. Our lives are full and complete only as all God's priorities are given their proper place.

What's the use of me standing up, preaching and teaching others, if I don't have a happy home and happy marriage — if I can't conduct my own affairs? So my message is developed as God's will is carried out in my life. If I'm always working for God, running to meetings, trying to be the perfect administrator, sitting in board meetings — and I don't have time for Bible study, for private prayers at length, or time to wait in the presence of God, what kind of a minister would I be? What message would I have?

God wants first of all to build my life before he wants to build a public ministry. My message is developed in a fruit-ful family relationship, in the daily routine of life and labor, so that I can take up my particular ministry that God has given me, and thereby be a blessing to the church.

Every man has a gift and it must be expressed. Personal application and effort must be made to build his own ministry. What God is trying to get across to us here is that before those extracurricular activities of our lives — pleasure moments, the hours spent in front of television, reading the extra book, or all sorts of other interesting things — take too much place in our lives we must take time to fulfill our ministry. Priorities often become jumbled.

One aspect of life can become so important to us that we completely neglect other matters. Establishing priorities makes it possible for us to make proper decisions on a day-to-day basis. It enables us to be happy, at peace, and productive.

The five priorities established in the word of God are the basis from which we can make major decisions when pressure is placed upon us. We are living in a day of pressure, when men don't know where to spend their time most fruitfully or productively. They don't know whether they should be at home, at work, at play, or at church.

Whatever the struggle you may be facing, God guarantees that if you will take His priority list and keep it in front of you when the decisions are made, you will discover that you'll be making them in favor of God's plan for your life. We cannot allow ourselves to be wife-controlled, family-controlled, job-controlled, or church-controlled if we are going to be productive. It all comes back to the very first issue of being spirit-controlled. It is then we will be able to cope with the other areas of priorities that God is concerned about. It is imperative that we come under the control of the Holy Spirit on a daily basis, spend time in prayer as Jesus did, and day by day he'll give us guidance as to the priorities for our lives.

May God help you and me to establish personal life priorities.

2

Marriage Misfits

Marriages are not all made in Heaven. To a great extent we either make or break them with our own hands.

These clumsy feet, still in the mire
Go crushing blossoms without end;
These hard, well meaning hands we thrust
Amid the heartstrings of a friend!

Happy marriages require some effort on both sides; they are neither accidental nor coincidental. Ruth Millett said, "Happy marriages are achieved by couples who consider each other's happiness as important as their own. Happy marriages are achieved by couples who know that love without mutual trust and respect doesn't last a lifetime."

We are faced with an increasing rate of unhappy marriages many of which are ending in divorce or disaster. An article in an old issue of Reader's Digest (1962), under the heading of "Wedlock Deadlock," set forth some candid questions with a very candid confession. Ask yourself these questions: "Is my marriage a success?" "Are my husband

and I compatible? "Did I marry the right man?" "Am I a good wife?"

One woman told me, "No. My marriage doesn't even qualify as a failure. It's a disaster." She was one of marriage's miserable misfits. It's a poor time to ask yourself if you've married the right man after nineteen years of marriage and when you are responsible for three children.

Marriage misfits are a result of:

A Careless Approach to Marriage; A Carefree Attitude Toward Marriage Obligations, and A Carousal Spirit After Marriage.

A Careless Approach to Marriage

Too many young people step into marriage with their eyes closed. They become infatuated and feel marriage is glamorous. Trusting everything to the romance of it all, they take a blind chance. What is forgotten is that marriage is for life and the romance stage can't last long. This is a careless approach to say the least.

Dr. R. Mace, speaking as executive director of the American Association of Marriage Counsellors, lay down some good advice when he said, "They . . . must decide what their policy about managing finances and dealing with property will be; what the standards and values, the religious attitudes they will jointly adopt will be. To plunge into marriage with major issues of this kind undecided is to add a mass of unfinished assignments to the already considerable tasks that settling down to married life involves."

In other words this is no move for a flighty, scatter-brained teenager who will not take the serious approach to life that marriage demands. Broken engagements are more the rule than the exception today, and that's a tell-tale sign. It's a sure thing that when a thousand cases reveal that one third of the men and half of the women had broken engagements, this generation is seized with a careless approach toward marriage.

Values, standards, and religious attitudes must be high on the list of unfinished business before a couple plunges into marriage. There must be mutual convictions about the permanency of marriage and the potency of religious beliefs. The scripture plainly states, "Be ye not unequally yoked together with unbelievers . . ." (II Corinthians 6:14). If you want to be added to the endless list of marriage misfits all you have to do is leave these issues undecided, or, compromise your convictions (and get the same result).

A friend once said, "Marriage is more than a verse of *O Promise Me,* confetti, and acknowledging a table full of gifts."

Dr. Mace told about one couple who came to him and admitted their marriage was empty, and for obvious reasons. "They had no religious belief that marriage is an indissoluble union. They didn't even feel that it was their social duty to remain married."

This careless approach to marriage is the cause of so many misfits simply because it is in violation of God's law and God's plan. "But from the beginning of the creation God made them male and female. For this cause shall a man leave his father and mother, and cleave to his wife; And they twain shall be one flesh: so then they are no more twain, but one flesh. What therefore God hath joined together, let not man put asunder" (Mark 10:6-9).

You become one flesh in the sight of God and no man or woman is to dissolve this union. Where is your fear of God? The apostle Paul urges all men to follow through with their vows when he states: "Submitting yourselves one to another in the fear of God. Wives, submit yourselves unto your own husbands, as unto the Lord. For the husband is the head of the wife, even as Christ is the head of the church . . ." (Ephesians 5:21-23).

It follows, that if you can't settle your religious views, or your convictions are incompatible, your marriage will be a misfit.

Marriage is not for children. One authority says, "More

and more girls are getting married too early. The consequences are frequently disastrous . . ." So it was in the case of Clarissa and Ralph when in less than a year he said, "I wish you were dead, because then I'd be free," and she slashed her wrists the same day. They were not ready for marriage at nineteen and sixteen years of age. They were misfits. Marriage misfits are a result of:

A Carefree Attitude Toward Marriage Obligations

"Marriage is a partnership. And yet it is the only partnership in the world where the details of the contract are not written down in black and white. It is a contract of trust based entirely on love." So states one great preacher, and thus reveals that every married couple have obligations to each other or, as the scripture says, ". . . neither is the man without the woman, neither the woman without the man . . ." (I Corinthians 11:11). First Corinthians 7:3 puts the emphasis on extreme courtesy when it says, "Let the husband render unto the wife due benevolence: and likewise also the wife unto the husband." We are to provide kindness and thoughtfulness along with the bread we bring home.

Don't forget that ". . . Man shall not live by bread alone . . ." (Matthew 4:4). Neither can a wife. She needs the love, understanding and protection that only you can give her. In return the dear wife should make herself worthy by continuing to be sweet, considerate and loveable. She is obliged to keep her hair done, some decent looking clothes on, and make herself attractive even after ten years of marriage. No man enjoys loving a has-been.

There should never be a carefree attitude that lets us feel, "Oh well, he's mine now, I have nothing to worry about." That attitude has forced many a marriage to the divorce courts.

We need to remember too that we leave our mother and father and cleave to one another. We don't run home every time the winds howl and the ship rocks a little. There is no room for asking Mom and Dad to look after us, or to subsidize our marriage. The obligations of marriage are to tough it together. One woman left her husband because she said, "He couldn't make a choice between his mother and me."

Set up a family altar, go to church, say prayers together — and when the going's tough, believe that the God who brought you together will keep you together. Set up a family altar and accept your obligations like a man. Someone has well said, "I'd sooner have a family altar than a family car." Marriage misfits arise all too frequently because neither one felt any spiritual obligation; neither one made a practice of going to the house of God. Children come along and you, having failed one another, fail them in your carefree attitude toward any spiritual obligations in your marriage. Get out on your own, face the storm, believe God and your marriage can never fail.

You are *obligated financially.* You must learn the first word in the marriage vocabulary is "ours" not "yours" or "mine." Your wife has as much right to the leisures of your income, if there are any, as you do. It's as hard to stay home, make beds, wash clothes, make meals and look after children as it is to go to work all day. We share our gains and our goods. Don't forget that we have obligations in marriage, and it's dangerous to be carefree about them. Accept them like a man. Marriage thrives on these things.

Take your union seriously and it will enhance your life; otherwise it will be as a great weight about your neck. Be ready to suffer a little for your partner's sake, be ready to share one another's interests and hobbies or give each other a night out. Talk like friends and take this thing seriously. It's a miserable thing to be a misfit when it comes to marriage, especially when it's simply because you were just too carefree about it all.

A Carousal Spirit After Marriage

Carousing after you've married can curse your relationship faster than any other thing. If you want to carouse, don't marry. If you are given to loose living, drink and shady friendships, don't marry. For marriage is dependent upon loyalty and fidelity. When you marry you must stop flirting, stop courting, and settle down to honest, wholesome living.

Some statistics released in the mid-1970s stated that more than thirty percent of children in the United States do not live with both of their natural parents. Absenteeism is both a fact of a crumbling society and an attitude of fathers toward their children.

Some people feel free to "carry-on" after entering into a marriage relationship. I heard, just recently, of a successful man coming home to find his wife in bed with another man. She had children to raise and a home to keep, but she was possessed with a carousal spirit.

How true the prophetic word of Jesus, when he said: "For as in the days that were before the flood they were eating and drinking, marrying and giving in marriage, until the day that Noah entered into the ark, And knew not until the flood came, and took them all away; so shall also the coming of the Son of man be" (Matthew 24:38,39).

The National Committee for Mental Hygiene tells us "the prevalence of sex experience outside of marriage is twice what it was thirty years ago."

Time Magazine has apty said, "Kinsey's work expresses and strengthens an attitude that can be dangerous: The idea that there is morality in numbers." (The thinking that because a lot of people do a particular thing that thing must be right.)

Watch that kind of reasoning. It will kill marriage. A woman is to be a "keeper at home," to be loyal and true while her man goes out to provide for her needs.

And to husbands I would say there is no room for excessive drinking, and night after night away with the boys. Beer and liquor call to you everywhere. Their advertising and suggestions are seductive, and before you know it, you will be doing what everybody else is doing. That's how it starts! Once the world pattern grips your home it moves quickly until climax follows climax and your home has gone the way of other homes. When you view the wreckage you ask yourself, "How did this happen?"

Let one party become charmed by a carousal spirit, and soon you'll see one staying by the home, and one out breaking the other's heart, while both become marriage misfits. Wake up before it's too late! Settle down to an honest Christian marriage. If carousing has played havoc with your life and marriage, follow the admonition of the great apostle who says, ". . . Awake thou that sleepest, and arise from the dead, and Christ shall give thee light" (Ephesians 5:14).

I know of nothing better than to ask you to dedicate your marriage and your home in a pattern suggested in paragraph 1935 in the Discipline of the Methodist Church, 1944:

We dedicate this home to the glory of God, committing to His loving care the house and all who dwell in it.

We dedicate this home to deep affections of the family circle, and to all friendly hospitalities.

We dedicate this home to all beautiful things of the heart and mind that lead the soul to wider vision and to higher aims.

We dedicate this home to happiness, to hopefulness, and to health, that it may ever be, to those whose home it is, a dear haven of peace and joy.

Don't let your marriage be a misfit . . ." *Be* kindly affectioned one to another . . ." (Romans 12:10). "Charity (love) never faileth" (I Corinthians 13:8).

3

Marriage and In-Laws

In-laws do not have to be out-laws. My in-laws have a warm place in my heart. I receive the finest treatment in their home right down to having my favorite dishes served when we arrive home for a visit. They gave me the best wife a man could ever have. My wife's mother trained her in household skills, taught her spiritual truth and took meticulous care for her development physically, mentally and spiritually. I respect my in-laws.

There are several instances in scripture that speak of kindness and compatibility between married couples and their in-laws. Ruth was a girl who grew to appreciate her husband's mother in a very special way. She learned to love her God and found salvation as a result. Peter's heart was moved on behalf of his wife's mother and he sought Jesus to come and heal her. It thrilled him to see her rise up and make a meal for the Master. Here is the story as recorded in Mark 1:30,31: "But Simon's wife's mother lay sick of a fever, and anon they tell him of her. And he came and took her by the hand, and lifted her up; and immediately the fever left her, and she ministered unto them."

Why is there so much friction with in-laws? Well, there are two sides to every story. Married couples often fail to accept their partner's parents and parents frequently find no place in their hearts for the new member in the family. Immaturity and selfishness in each case is the cause of the trouble. If you have been blessed with a good wife then it's likely because she had a good home. You are not marrying her parents but you owe them the same amount of respect they receive from their daughter. The same rule applies for both parties. God's word teaches us to "Honour thy father and mother; which is the first commandment with promise; That it may be well with thee . . ." (Ephesians 6:2,3). Remember this kind of reverence doesn't end when we get married. Mutual respect must prevail. Parents must treat both children as their own, for the Bible says that they are "one flesh" (Mark 10:8).

Another big in-law problem arises when one party disregards the scripture that teaches us, "Therefore shall a man leave his father and mother . . ." (Genesis 2:24). When a couple marries they learn to tough it together. They don't take their troubles home to Mom and Dad or keep crying the blues about all their problems. They don't seek sympathy from their relatives. They must learn to work things out on their own, accepting their lot in life and seeking the grace of God to help in time of need.

It might be suggested that most in-laws fall into three categories: *The intruder; the indifferent, and the inspiring.*

In-Laws Who Intrude

Some people just do not know how to stay out of other people's affairs. If your marriage has been cursed with in-laws who will not let you live your own lives I suggest you avoid them as much as possible. I don't advocate ignoring them, just have no more to do with them than is necessary. Try not to antagonize them and if they insist on meddling, ask them to kindly let you work out your own problems.

Proverbs 15:1 says, "A soft answer turneth away wrath: but grievous words stir up anger." Avoid stirring up trouble in either family if it is at all possible.

Jacob had the unfortunate experience of living with his father-in-law and found him to be an intruder of the worst sort. I pity the couple that has to live in the same house with their in-laws. It is so easy for in-laws to take sides, or else pass along "free" advice, and usually they create a difficult situation. Jacob had it rough. He lived on the same farm with his father-in-law and for fourteen years suffered from one intrusion after another. He and his wife finally felt they had taken enough so moved out and away. *"Is there* yet any portion or inheritance for us in our father's house? Are we not counted of him strangers? for he hath sold us, and hath quite devoured also our money. For all the riches which God hath taken from our father, that *is* ours, and our children's: now then, whatsoever God hath said unto thee, do. Then Jacob rose up, and . . . fled" (Genesis 31:14-17,21).

Intruders into your marriage should be treated as such in order to save it from disaster. You must not be afraid to take action, or drastic measures, if it is in favor of your happy home.

In-Laws Who are Indifferent

Some people just do not seem to care what happens to their children. They do not seem to have any time for their family. There are times when we need each other and we should learn this important fact of life. Lot learned this lesson far too late. He neglected his family and later tried to influence them only to be mocked in disrespect. This story is written in Genesis 19:14: "And Lot went out, and spake unto his sons in law, which married his daughters, and said, Up, get you out of this place; for the Lord will destroy this city. But he seemed as one that mocked unto his sons in law."

When parents fail to show an interest in their married

children they very soon lose their confidence.

There are many reasons why parents grow indifferent toward their grown family and these reasons are worth our consideration. For example, some young people live so much to themselves, and get so taken up with each other, that they make their folks feel unwanted. They have no time to write, no time to visit and no interest in anything, or any one, but themselves. If you don't take a little interest, take the new babies over to see Grandma and Grandpa, or let them know how things are with your family, then don't be surprised if indifference prevails. It's the principle of Proverbs 18:24, "A man *that hath* friends must shew himself friendly . . ." Family love, like all true love, is usually reciprocal by nature.

Indifference will sometimes prevail because of sulking (or sick) parents. There have been children who married contrary to the will and express desire of their elders and, as a result, they have been virtually disowned. The parents have become so displeased that they sulk and refuse to have anything to do with their own offspring. This is childish and often very foolish.

I used the term sick advisedly as I relate it in some cases to the sin of drunkenness. In-laws who are given to alcohol cannot help but be indifferent toward their married children for they are sick at heart. For "Who hath woe? who hath sorrow? who hath contentions? who hath babbling? who hath wounds without cause? who hath redness of eyes? They that tarry long at the wine; they that go to seek mixed wine" (Proverbs 23:29,30).

Mutual interest and respect, in spite of failures, sins or shortcomings, are the only answers to a harmonious relationship between in-laws. Both sides must make an honest effort.

In-Laws Who Inspire

We have considered two extreme conditions that can

develop and now would like to discuss the ideal situation. If parents act wisely they can be a real help and inspiration to their married children. My wife and I have been greatly encouraged and inspired by our good parents on both sides. There is no doubt that Ruth felt the same way when she said to her mother-in-law, ". . . Intreat me not to leave thee, *or* to return from following after thee: for whither thou goest, I will go; and where thou lodgest, I will lodge: thy people *shall be* my people, and thy God my God: Where thou diest, will I die, and there will I be buried: the Lord do so to me, and more also, *if ought* but death part thee and me" (Ruth 1:16,17).

It's a thrill to have a godly example to follow; a law of kindness to encourage us and prayers to strengthen the heart in times of trial and testing. When young couples see that we care, and that we are willing to help out at times, it gives them a real lift. Maybe it's to back a loan, or advance them some needed cash, or offer to take the children for a spell, or present them with an exciting gift on their wedding day. Let me suggest that it is just a case of doing as Solomon admonished when he wrote, "Withhold not good from them to whom it is due, when it is in the power of thine hand to do *it*" (Proverbs 3:27).

It's not a matter of handouts but of common kindness toward our own flesh and blood. If there is not much to offer then give them what must go with every gift, your heart in love and affection. Let me leave you with these final words as written by Dr. C. M. Ward. "It is too easy to turn 'in-laws' into 'out-laws' who prey upon your marriage. *Your relatives are precious friends but not partners.* Use the needed tact to make their friendship deep and true." These words of wisdom apply equally to married couples and their parents. We need each other and we need God.

Marriage Lines

At first we drew between us
A sharp, distinctive line,

And all was yours on that side,
And all on this was mine.

Your hopes, your fears, your friendships
(Your money, too, my dear),
Were neatly on the far side
And mine, as neatly, here.

But years have dimmed the marking,
The line has lost its powers.
Now everything is mingled,
Now yours and mine are "Ours."

Richard Armour

4

Marriage and Money

Marriage management is no small matter. When you leave home and set out upon the sea of matrimony you are also embarking upon a big business. Money is important, but you'll never know to what extent until you have a home to keep and a family to feed. Marriage is expensive and you should not plan such a move without considerable preparation. You will soon find out that money does not make a marriage but it can break one. You can start out on a shoe string but be very careful not to pull it too tight. If you start out in a small way you must be content to get along on the bare necessities and not allow yourselves too many luxuries.

Here is how one author put it: "Desires for luxuries and a higher standard of living, will increase as quickly, if not more quickly, than your increased prosperity. Savings before marriage is a must."

It takes money to provide for a wife and family and the scripture says, "But if any provide not for his own, and specially for those of his own house, he hath denied the faith, and is worse than an infidel" (I Timothy 5:8).

We have now established the important part money plays in marriage and we will go on to discuss it in more detail, but before we do, remember, "Money is a universal provider of everything but happiness; and a passport to everywhere but heaven."

Here now are three things to note about marriage and money:

Start by taking out the tithe for God;
Steer clear of damaging debt, and
Settle which partner will manage the money.

Taking Out the Tithe for God

One sure way to succeed in any business is to take God in as your partner, and by giving Him his rightful portion you do exactly that. Everything we have is a gift of God and all He asks in return is one tenth of our income. As our partner He works with us and for us as we acknowledge Him in this matter. "Bring ye all the tithes into the storehouse, that there may be meat in mine house, and prove me now herewith, saith the Lord of hosts, if I will not open you the windows of heaven, and pour you out a blessing, that *there shall* not *be room* enough *to receive it*" (Malachi 3:10). This is, as one man says, "A spiritual law that is a foundation for financial success."

"Honour the Lord with thy substance, and with the firstfruits of all thine increase:" and if you will — here is the promise, "So shall thy barns be filled with plenty, and thy presses shall burst out with new wine" (Proverbs 3:9,10).

Now you don't have to follow this pattern of giving to God first, but when you do, all other things are added. "But seek ye first the kingdom of God, and his righteousness (in your marriage) and all these things shall be added unto you" (Matthew 6:33). "Give, and it shall be given unto you; good measure, pressed down, and shaken together, and running over, shall men give into your bosom" (Luke 6:38).

Young people who start their marriage on the tithing principle make themselves candidates for the fullness of God's abundance. "All things" are taken care of through the providing hand of the Lord. If the Lord has brought you together He is surely able to meet your needs. Financial pressures will plague you at times but if you have honored God in your giving, you have a claim upon his provisions and promises. "But my God shall supply all your need according to his riches in glory by Christ Jesus" (Philippians 4:19).

Tithing, too, is the first step in learning how to use money wisely. So many marriages teeter on the verge of bankruptcy because of unwise spending. Invest first in the kingdom of God, then seek divine wisdom in handling your income. "If any of you lack wisdom, let him ask of God" (James 1:5) the scriptures tell us, and it certainly applies in this matter of money in marriage.

One writer has well said, "The man who has mastered the art of wisely using his money, and who obeys the laws of God in this regard, is well on his road to success." Marriage is one business that must succeed, and one sure way to attain this success in the financial realm is to say as Jacob did when starting out on his own, ". . . and of all that thou shalt give me I will surely give the tenth unto thee" (Genesis 28:22). This approach will keep you from the cancer of covetousness that curses so many happy homes. Some couples never have enough. We all need to learn the lesson the great apostle Paul learned. Hear his testimony: ". . . I have learned, in whatsoever state I am, *therewith* to be content" (Philippians 4:11). He was contented, not covetous, not complaining, not clamoring, for he believed that "godliness with contentment is great gain" (I Timothy 6:6).

I repeat, therefore, that putting ten percent of your money out for use in the kingdom of God is a sound spiritual approach when it comes to handling money in marriage.

We have never known what it was to have extra money in our home but we certainly have enjoyed God's goodness in providing for our needs. It has been a real joy to have shared in giving to the extension of the kingdom of God out of that which the Lord has given us. Share what you have with God, seek His wisdom in your spending, and you'll never be in want.

Steer Clear of Damaging Debt

It has been said that if we are to succeed in life there are three things we must avoid — dirt, debt, and the devil. Here is a threatening threesome. Any one of this trio could destroy a happy marriage. I fear debt as much as any of them and the Bible plainly states, "Owe no man any thing" (Romans 13:8). I won't say that I am against buying articles on time, but this "dollar-down-and-dollar-a-week" philosophy can create a lot of damaging debt.

What is the difference between buying on time and damaging debt? This is something you can find out if you don't learn to spend within the boundaries of your income. You can make payments on a monthly basis, meet those payments and never run into trouble, but if you start making purchases that strain your income you have damaging debt. It can be a good thing to have established a credit rating in your community, yet it can be harmful to have failed in meeting your payments.

The Rev. G.F. Atter expresses this thought extremely well: "While it is generally advisable to avoid going into debt, there are times when some things which are essential can only be purchased through credit buying. At such times it is a great advantage to have a good credit rating, either at a bank or at a reliable store or insurance company. The practice of thrift over a period of years, the reputation of always paying bills promptly and the fact of having acquired collateral, all help to establish sound credit in a community. Hence, there are occasions when the fact you have previously borrowed money, and satisfactorily repaid the loan, becomes a definite asset."

Don't spend beyond your ability to pay. Don't acquire a

rich taste unless you can afford it. Don't expect your parents to subsidize you after you have bought foolishly. The Bible says we are to "leave . . . father and mother" (Genesis 2:24), and that means we are not to expect them to support our marriage for us.

Dr. Lee Burchinal, in his Iowa researches of young marriages, found that only one third of the couples he studied could maintain a separate home of their own. When a man decides to get married he is saying, "Look, I can now stand on my own two feet, support a wife and raise a family." To do that, a young man must steer clear of debt and do without many comforts and luxuries. These commodities only come to most of us after years of toil and thrift and, as one marriage counsellor put it, "I know that working hard and sacrificing to establish a home and to provide for children is almost never the cause of a broken marriage. On the contrary, many couples admit that such shared effort has bound them into a deeper and more lasting comradeship."

Sacrifices are generally necessary and debt must be avoided if at all possible. As long as both parties are willing to forego luxury and are ready to work hard they can make a successful marriage with or without an abundance of money. Anything that is worth having is worth working for, and that is true in marriage as much as anything else in life. Jacob worked for fourteen years before he finally took the wife he wanted in his life. I don't advocate waiting that long or saving that long, but don't marry if you have to plunge yourself into debt to do so.

Who Will Manage the Money?

Every good business has one major manager and so does every good marriage. Settle this point before you marry. "Can two walk together, except they be agreed?" (Amos 3:3). Decide who has the best business head in the family. Decide on a budget and on your banking system. These are all good matters to clear up before you get involved in the further complications of life. You should calculate your income and expenses and then figure out a budget. If you can't do it alone ask someone who can help you.

Often a woman is endowed with a capacity for thrift, and happy is the man who finds such a woman. Solomon states it like this, "Who can find a virtuous woman? for her price *is* far above rubies. The heart of her husband doth safely trust in her, so that he shall have no need of spoil. She will do him good and not evil all the days of her life." Notice how thrifty she is: "She considereth a field, and buyeth it." That means she compares prices and spends wisely. She is a good manager or as Solomon further remarks, "She perceiveth that her merchandise *is* good . . ." (Proverbs 31:10-12,16,18).

One partner must manage the funds and it must be with mutual agreement. Settle the matter of management and let there be no austerity or lordship over the funds on the part of the one who handles them. Let there be allowances made for the necessities and pastimes of both parties. Some marriages are not short of money but too often only one partner is enjoying all the benefits. It matters a great deal how money is handled. Each should have a small private allowance from which to purchase that anniversary gift or some other little nicety of life. Remember it is "our" income and not "mine."

Mismanagement can be disastrous. You can have a good income but if you squander it you can be in trouble. I once had an acquaintance who made some of the biggest money to be had in his town yet he never had one thing to show for it and his family suffered. Did he drink or gamble? No, he just spent his money on unnecessary commodities. He held the money but it never performed its duty for that family. Why should one party be allowed to go out and spend money on articles before the family has a good home to live in? Why should we accumulate things while our family puts up with inadequate living quarters?

Settle on who will manage the money and if it is not working out, then review your approach to this issue. One bank manager made this suggestion. "Review your budget plan . . . to find whether you are moving ahead, or slipping behind. Don't be easily discouraged if you fail at the beginning to adhere strictly to the plan. You will succeed if you are determined to succeed."

In Proverbs 3:6, we read, In all thy ways acknowledge him, and he shall direct thy paths."

5

Love, Marriage and the Sanctity of Sex

There are shocking revelations of a serious moral breakdown in our society and the increasing number of sex symbols and sex queens is one of the many reflections of this problem. In spite of the glaring facts, let me say that there is still something sacred about sex. We have taken this sacred gift of God and wrapped it in the tinsel of some weak symbol and destroyed its true meaning and purpose. The words love, virginity, and holy matrimony still have deep meaning to most of us, and we resent this degrading presentation of morality and sex. Love, marriage and sex go together, and apart from the marriage relationship, sex is stripped of all its true meaning.

In his answer to the Kinsey report, Billy Graham said, "Sex relations, stripped of mutual love, respect, and the sincere desire to give joy and fulfillment within the holy bonds of matrimony, degenerate into the lowest form of immorality." Morals are not relative, they are absolute. The Bible is the true standard for all moral codes and the Bible says that sex belongs to marriage.

Jesus said, "But from the beginning of the creation God

made them male and female. For this cause shall a man leave his father and mother, and cleave to his wife; And they twain shall be one flesh: so then they are no more twain, but one flesh. What therefore God hath joined together, let not man put asunder" (Mark 10:6-9).

The Bible teaching and the statements of men like Dr. Granville Fisher, a Miami psychologist, are in no way compatible. Dr. Fisher said, "Sex is not a moral question. For answers you don't turn to the body of absolutes. The criterion cannot be, is it morally right or wrong, but, is it socially feasible, is it personally healthy and rewarding, will it enrich human life." He is dead wrong, and this kind of teaching is completely incongruous with scripture, therefore, must be rejected.

Jesus made it very plain. It is a matter of right and wrong, regardless of how rewarding we find our sinful acts. That measure of enjoyment does not make it right. The truth is that *"when it (sin) is finished, (it) bringeth forth death"* (James 1:15).

To accept such philosophy as men are expressing, is to reject the ten commandments and to reject the sermon on the mount; one given by God and the other presented by Jesus Christ His Son. If Dr. Fisher is right when he said of protestant clergymen, "They are no longer shaking their finger because boys and girls give in to urges and experiment a bit. They don't say, stop you're wrong, but, is it meaningful?" If this is true, then woe is unto us.

I will lend my voice to the need of the hour, and will go on record as standing true to the word of God. God's word tells me all this sexual promiscuity is totally wrong. The commandment declares, "Thou shalt not commit adultery" (Exodous 20:14). Time nor trends cannot alter this irrevocable law of God in any way. Jesus added His comment to that commandment with these words, "Ye have heard that it was said by them of old time, Thou shalt not commit adultery: But I say unto you, That whosoever looketh on a woman to lust after her hath committed adultery with her already in his heart" (Matthew 5:27,28). Adultery and fornication are still sin, and Galatians 5:19, 21 speaks of this as works of the flesh. "Now the works of the flesh are manifest, which are *these;* Adultery, fornication, uncleanness, lasciviousness . . . of the which I tell you before, as I have also told *you* in time past, that they which do such things shall not inherit the kingdom of God." Adultery and fornication are serious sins that can bar you from the kingdom of God, and lead your soul into hell. Yes, a hell on earth as well as a destruction hereafter.

If you think it is rewarding, and you can get meaning out of indulging in such sinful acts, then you should talk to the multitudes whose sins have found them out. I don't care if everyone is doing it. That doesn't make it right, and neither does it take care of the painful hours of remorse that so often follow.

What of the illegitimate children and the scorching guilt complex that has almost overwhelmed so many young people? You can't sin and get away with it, for the Bible plainly states, ". . . be sure your sin will find you out" (Numbers 32:23). Illegitimacy is still the major problem.

According to Planned Parenthood — World Population, a Washington D.C. based organization, about a million American teenagers a year become pregnant, and about 200,000 give birth to out-of-wedlock children. Having babies out of wedlock is no mean matter. You just have to talk with an unwed mother to realize the many hours of remorse she faces; to say nothing of the loneliness and depression she feels.

Once a college problem, premarital pregnancy has become a highschool problem. The U.S. Centre for National Statistics states that in one year, more than a million teens, one out of every eleven girls between the ages of 14 and 19 had become pregnant.

I wonder if Solomon's picture of an adulterous woman is not a picture of our adulterous generation when he writes, "Such *is* the way of an adulterous woman; she eateth, and wipeth her mouth, and saith, I have done no wickedness" (Proverbs 30:20). It seems to be a very vivid protrayal of our times when you read that a recent poll conducted by a leading women's journal reveals that ninety percent of middle class women surveyed under the age of twenty-five had engaged in premarital sex. God's word still warns our young people to "Flee also youthful lusts . . ." (II Timothy 2:22), and particularly commands us to "Flee fornication. Every sin that a man doeth is without the body; but he that committeth fornication sinneth against his own body" (I Corinthians 6:18).

The crisis of virginity is no longer considered to be a serious matter in the view of a high percentage of the populace. The loss of virginity even resulting in pregnancy, is simply no longer considered an American tragedy. One student says this of the American vernacular, "The word virgin is taking on a slightly new meaning. It seems acceptable to consider a girl a virgin if she has had experience with only her husband before marriage, or with only one or two steadies."

This definition falls far short of the Bible standard for girls or guys. The Bible admonishes ". . . keep thyself pure" (I Timothy 5:22). Let it also be known that Jesus put a premium on purity, saying, "Blessed (or happy) *are* the pure in heart: for they shall see God" (Matthew 5:8). Purity still has its premium and girls should see that they maintain it, while fellows should learn to respect its value in this life.

My father sat down with me one day to have a fatherly talk about sex and what he said followed me all the days of my life. He said, "Son, never do anything to any girl you wouldn't want done to your own sister." Those words rang in my ears and penetrated into my soul to become a constant safeguard against evil. Girls should have a deep sense of self-respect, and fellows should show them the same amount of respect they would show for their sisters or mothers.

Purity is not some cheap commodity picked up on the bargain counters of our land, but it is still an all-preserving power in any society where it is maintained. It is rewarding, for only those with a pure heart can enter the presence of the Lord. "Who shall ascend into the hill of the Lord? or who shall stand in his holy place? He that hath clean hands, and a pure heart; who hath not lifted up his soul unto vanity, nor sworn deceitfully" (Psalm 24:3,4). Purity or virginity is not as some would have it. Webster defines it like this: "Freedom from guilt or the defilement of sin; innocence; chastity. Freedom from foreign admixture or deleterious matter. Cleanness; freedom from foulness or dirt. Freedom from any sinister or improper motives or views."

It's no wonder the scripture says, "But fornication, and all uncleanness, or covetousness, let it not be once named among you, as becometh saints" (Ephesians 5:3); and again, "Mortify therefore your members which are upon the earth; fornication, uncleanness, inordinate affection, evil concupiscence, and covetousness, which is idolatry: For which things' sake the wrath of God cometh on the children of disobedience" (Colossians 3:5,6).

So in spite of all moral breakdowns let us strive to retain the highest standard possible. There are stories told in the United States of non-virgin clubs in highschools. In order to be a member, virginity must be violated. I call upon each of you to take your stand on the other side of the fence, and to divorce yourselves from all such impurities. "I can do all things through Christ which strengtheneth me" (Philippians 4:13), the apostle Paul declared. We have his promise in II Timothy 4:18, "And the Lord shall deliver me from every evil work, and will preserve *me* unto his heavenly kingdom: to whom *be* glory for ever and ever."

God can keep us until we enter into holy matrimony where sex finds its true meaning. There is nothing unholy about sex when it is sanctified by marriage. It then becomes a very sacred thing. It is to be entered into by married couples as an expression of love. Mutual giving is involved. You do not defraud or withhold yourself from one another. Personal feelings of coolness, tiredness, or indifference do not come between you and the desires of your partner. Mutuality is the key word in marriage. Consideration is your major concern. Courtesy comes first when approaching sex in marriage.

Too long have married couples been selfishly motivated. Some are overbearing, some are absolutely frigid and unfair, and some seek only to be satisfied and not to give satisfaction. I Corinthians 7:2-5, from Williams translation makes this thought very clear when it says; "Because of so much sexual immorality every man should have a wife of his own, and every woman a husband of her own. The husband must always give his wife what is due her, and the wife too must do so for the husband. The wife does not have the right to do as she pleases with her own body; the husband has his right to it. You husbands and wives must stop refusing each other what is due, unless you just agree to do so just for a while, so as to have plenty of time for prayer, and then to be together again, so as to keep satan from tempting you because of your lack of self-control."

This portion makes it plain that sex belongs in marriage, and marriage only. If there was more time in the lives of married couples for such mutual love and respect there would be less marriages going on the rocks. Immorality can spoil the enjoyment of the highest and best in the true marriage relationship. Albert Curry Winn said: "You may be slick as a whistle in avoiding venereal disease or pregnancy, but there is no defence against spiritual venereal disease, the insidious damage that comes to a man's soul when he abuses God's gift of sexual power with someone other than his true partner."

First Corinthians 6:16 says, "Do you know that he who joins himself to a prostitute becomes one body with her?" Whether you want to or not, you do. And every experience of that kind lessens, by so much, the unity that will be possible between you and your mate. You will never wholly belong to that wife you dream of because you left part of yourself with the girl who gave you an hour's pleasure. The modern mentality toward morality would not agree with such philosophy, but real life and God's word certainly would agree. This kind of article would confirm what John Meldau once wrote, "Free love, trial marriage, nudism, adultery, fornication, bestiality, polygamy, promiscuity, and all manner of sordid sensuality are here; immorality is spreading like a prairie fire. Men are trying desperately to be rid of puritanical taboos and the moral codes of the scriptures."

It has once been stated, "The Victorians who talked a great deal about love, knew little about sex. Perhaps it is time that modern Americans who know a great deal about sex, once again start talking about love."

There are two words for love: "eros," which is based alone on the passions, and "agape," which is the purest form of the passions or of love itself. One statement made by a theologian will help add the true emphasis needed in our time. "Eros is accorded high rank today, 'a rank that comes close to the deity it once had.' The spiritual danger is the eros may leave no room for agape, which lives not by making claims but by giving."

We need this true love with its twelve characteristics as outlined in Philips translation of I Corinthians 13.

This love is:

Slow to lose patience.
It looks for a way of being constructive.
It is not possessive.
It is not anxious to impress.
It does not cherish inflated ideas of its own importance.
It is not touchy.
It does not gloat over the wickedness of others.
It is glad with all good men when truth prevails.
Love knows no limits to its endurance.
No end to its trust.
No fading to its hope.
It can outlast anything. It is, in fact, the one thing that still stands when all else has fallen.

6

Warning to an Adulterous Generation: The Seventh Commandment

The seventh commandment, having to do with chastity and purity could never be uttered at a more opportune time. We live in a day when virtue is a lost art, impurity hardly receives a frown, and illegitimacy is hardly considered a misfortune. God still hates this sin, and it receives His severest judgment. He also pronounces judgment upon those who practice it. Hebrews 13:4 says, ". . . whoremongers and adulterers God will judge." This text cannot help but arrive home to a generation that is facing one of the greatest moral breakdowns in modern history.

In three California counties there are more divorces than marriages. In the state of California it is reported that fifteen to twenty-five percent of all youth do not know who their fathers are.

Adultery is primarily a crime against the marriage relationship. It used to be that only the odd North American home was broken because of adultery, but today it has become common and shameless. At one time, only the odd, loose-living person was caught in illegitimacy, but today it is nothing to find a nurse, a lab technician, a school teacher, or even a fine, upstanding mother in the community snared by this sin of adultery. I think of one woman I know, an outstanding woman who has been living common-law, or in open adultery, for some years now and has never lost her status in the eyes of the community. "A victim of circumstances," you might say . . . I say, a victim of sin, and sin's hellish hold on the soul.

Adultery — Its Character

What is the character of adultery? How is this sin committed? Is it by the direct act alone? Let us consider it's character in the light of scripture.

Adultery is impurity of heart. Matthew 5:28 says, "But I say unto you, That whosoever looketh on a woman to lust after her hath committed adultery with her already in his heart." Jesus always went a step further than the ancient law. He here demands purity of heart as much as purity of conduct. Second Peter 2:14 speaks of "eyes full of adultery." According to Jesus, we are involved in this sin as soon as we look on a woman and begin to harbor evil thoughts, evil purposes or evil affections. It says of Noah's generation that " . . . God saw that the wickedness of man *was* great in the earth, and *that* every imagination of the thoughts of his heart *was* only evil continually (Genesis 6:5), and "they did marry and did give in marriage or divorced."

This means that you have no right to "eye" a girl up and down as though she belonged to you; and if and when you do, you have broken the seventh commandment that says, "Thou shalt not commit adultery" (Exodus 20:14).

The sin of the eye involving a man or woman in adultery carries into the realm of reading and pornography. Melton Wright, in an article called "Sin in our Magazines," made these comments: "In the not too distant past, one had to get magazines of a dubious nature from under the counter or from a shady neighborhood character who would stoop to anything to make a dime. Not so today! If (a man) wants to acquire pornographic magazines or sexy, sadistic and salacious literature, he only has to visit the corner drug-store, or neighborhood newsstand and he can see and read about sins that great grandfather never dreamed in inno-cent little Hometown, U.S.A."

In one magazine with a fairly conservative home reputa-tion, stories contained twenty-five references to smoking, seven to adultery, three to divorce, and sixteen to curses and lewd remarks. One story was about a man who tried to steal another man's wife, a second told of a married man's affair with his secretary, a third had a wife kill her husband because she learned he was having a clandestine affair with another woman, and a fourth was very suggestively written. From this it is quite evident that adultery, as Jesus defines it, can be committed by reading or by dwelling on the litera-ture that we have all around us today.

Adultery can result from impure words. Ephesians 4:29 says, "Let no corrupt communication proceed out of your mouth . . ." Again in Ephesians 5:4,5 we read, "Neither filthiness, nor foolish talking, nor jesting, which are not convenient . . . For this ye know, that no whoremonger, nor unclean person . . . hath any inheritance in the kingdom of Christ and of God."

There seems to be a strong implication here that filthy talking and jesting can involve a person in adultery in the sight of God. The reason would seem to be that God knows what's in a man's heart when his speech is unclean. The dirty joke, careless and crude talk about the opposite sex, cunning remarks, and many, many other such things which could be classed as filthy communications can involve us in this sin of adultery.

Adultery is also impure actions. This commandment taken in its most literal form, forbids the overt act of adultery implicating two persons. In conversing with one person about this text he boldly asked me, as though sure of the

answer before he asked, "How many keep this commandment today?"

That is a fair question! Common-law living is appalling,
the number of broken homes is alarming, and the reported
sexual relationships before marriage are awful.

Adultery was the act that crippled David, crushed
Samson, and condemned the woman at the well. It was this
gross act that ministered the final blow in each case but
there were, and always are, other acts leading up to the
final breakdown. There is the act of impudent and light
behavior, and immodest gestures such as we read about in
Isaiah, "Moreover the Lord saith, Because the daughters of
Zion are haughty, and walk with stretched forth necks and
wanton eyes, walking and mincing *as* they go, and making a
tinkling with their feet" (Isaiah 3:16).

Here the Lord pictures women who dress and walk in a
suggestive or provocative manner. These actions provoke
the ultimate act forbidden in the seventh commandment,
and are forbidden with the same degree of severity. It's important that we refrain from indecent dress, immoral
actions, immodest posture, the pampering of the flesh on
the dance floor, and the premature necking on some back
road, so as not to provoke this sin. For it says of the harlot in
Proverbs 7:13, "So she caught him, and kissed him, *and* with
an impudent face said unto him, *I have* peace offerings with
me . . ." and all other such actions have a strong tendency to
implicate us in this sin of adultery.

Adultery — Its Consequences

The consequences of this sin might seem self-evident,
yet it will prove to be a strong deterrent to enumerate results
as they are in the scriptures. All who would allow themselves to become a victim of this sin ought to first consider
the ultimate consequences.

First, it dishonors and debases the body. First Corinthians 6:18 says, "Flee fornication. Every sin that a man doeth is without the body; but he that committeth fornication sinneth against his own body." When we become involved in illicit sex, we sin against our body. The person who has been victimized in this way has done his or her body an injustice. Who wants to enter into matrimony with a defiled body? Who, especially one of the male sex, wants to receive a defiled body? Remember that it's really worth something to do as Timothy says, "keep thyself pure" (I Timothy 5:22).

A Greek maid, being asked what fortune she would bring her husband, answered, "I will bring him what is more valuable than any treasure — a heart unspotted, a virtue without a stain, which is all that descended to me from my parents."

No woman could have a more valuable dowry! If you are a professed child of God, your body is a "temple of the Holy Ghost" (I Corinthians 6:19). You are not your own when you have been bought with the precious blood of Christ. Be careful how you treat your body.

Second, adultery leaves an indelible stain upon the reputation. Proverbs 6:33 says, "A wound and dishonour shall he get; and his reproach shall not be wiped away."

Society may have come to accept the adulterer and the adulteress but they still carry the stain of a sordid reputation in their souls — a reproach that "shall not be wiped away." This sin brings dishonor to the family name and to the family reputation, and the reproach is indelible. Society might forget, but the soul is forever stained and the memory is forever singed.

". . . sin *is* a reproach to any people," Proverbs 14:34 says. You can repent, but never escape the reproach of this sin. David is a classic example of a man who fell into this trap and his sin has never been wiped away. Recently a film was made that exploits David's sin, and Samson's as well. Remember this, the world never forgets! There was a time when more was made of the reproach, and that was a good day — when fellows and girls thought of the dishonor and reproach attached to premarital sex and it was a deterrent.

Third, poverty and want ofttimes follow. Proverbs 5:8-10 reads, "Remove thy way far from her, and come not nigh the door of her house: Lest thou give thine honour unto others, and thy years unto the cruel: Lest strangers be filled with thy wealth; and thy labours *be* in the house of a stranger." Again we read, "For by means of a whorish woman *a man is brought* to a piece of bread" (Proverbs 6:26). Much of a man's wealth can be eaten away when he becomes ensnared by adultery. It is, to the man who is trapped, what the sin of drunkenness is to the man who is bound by drink. It takes a man's money, his time, and his health.

Fourth, it is a sin that can damn the soul. Again we read in Proverbs 6:32, *"But* whoso committeth adultery with a woman lacketh understanding: he *that* doeth it destroyeth his own soul."

Surely adultery is a crime! However silent our laws may be, let us never forget that God is not silent. The Bible does not whisper; it thunders peal on peal the hot denunciations of divine wrath against the adulterer. Proverbs 7:27 speaks of the way of adultery as being ". . . the way to hell, going down to the chambers of death." Job 31:11 calls it "an heinous crime; yea, it *is* an iniquity *to be punished by* the judges."

So the denunciation and damnation attached to the sin of adultery is very clear and calculated throughout the Word of God.

Adultery — Its Cure

There are probably many cures that could be mentioned here, but I would like to suggest some that I feel are very important. Of course, the only real cure for those who have been caught either in act or thought is the Blood of Jesus Christ. First John 1:7 reads, ". . . the blood of Jesus Christ his Son cleanseth us from all sin." There is one cure for every sin-stained soul and that is the blood of Jesus Christ, the divine detergent. ". . . though your sins be as scarlet, they shall be as white as snow; though they be red like crimson, they shall be as wool" (Isaiah 1:18). Salvation is the only lasting cure for the sin of adultery and it is available to all men.

Some of the other cures I might mention could fall into the category of preventatives, such as:

Guard your thoughts and what you watch and read. Philippians 4:8 admonishes, "Finally, brethren, whatsoever things are true, whatsoever things *are* honest, whatsoever things *are* just, whatsoever things *are* pure, . . . *are* lovely . . . of good report; if *there be* any virtue . . . think on these things." One sure way to keep ourselves from becoming victimized is to shun the evil thoughts that dash themselves across the mind; shun the evil conversation of our day, and shun the filthy literature on the newsstands.

Guard against evil company and be modest in your attire. How you dress and what you wear might be very important to you. It is also of utmost importance what company you choose and the companions you go out with. A young woman should not allow herself to become the tool of some lewd fellows. A young man should not let some flattering filly cast her lot on his doorstep.

There was a girl in our town who had the reputation for trapping her prey and she managed to throw many a strong man to his shame and disgrace. To be seen with her was considered extremely bad taste. And, you know that you have used poor judgment when you take up with a disreputable character.

Beware of pampering the flesh and excess diet. If you want to deliver yourself from this trap, shun the dance floors where passions are let loose, and so is hell. Keep yourself from drink and overindulgences.

Just recently I heard of a lab technician who, up until the time she took an overdose of liquor, was pure and unspotted. But, after she had become somewhat inebriated she ended up with an illegitimate child, pain, sorrow, a mess of trouble, and a whole lot of heartache. I know of another woman, who had just buried her husband (the mayor of that small town) when she was overtaken by alcohol. From that one night's excess, she bore the shame, sorrow, and hell of an illegitimate child. Eight months passed before she even saw a doctor. All that time, she bore the pains of hell in her soul. So, one sure cure is to keep your appetites under control.

Labour to get the fear of God in your hearts and to walk in the Spirit. ". . . by the fear of the Lord *men* depart from evil" (Proverbs 16:6). The best preventative of the works of the flesh is to "be filled with the Spirit" and the best pattern toward purity is to "walk in the Spirit" as listed in Ephesians 5:8-18 and Galatians 5:16-21.

The baptism of the Holy Spirit will give you power to combat an unholy spirit, the power to resist the tempting parking place, and the power to pray. If you desire to be pure and keep clean, be "filled with the Spirit" of God.

7

Havoc in the Home

God's Word is plain in telling us that He instituted marriage, family life and the home, but, like many other blessed institutions of God, some men have made havoc of the home. They have failed to recognize the home for what it really is, a creation of God.

The devil has attacked the home with all the ferocity of a wild beast. No wonder Peter warned us by saying, "Be sober, be vigilant; because your adversary the devil, as a roaring lion, walketh about, seeking whom he may devour: Whom resist stedfast in the faith . . ." (I Peter 5:8, 9). Satan is out to undermine the stability of the home. He knows that this is the heart of our society. Do you know what is causing so much havoc in the modern home? Let me suggest three main sources that contribute to this problem.

The Problem of Drink.

It has been stated that in the course of a lifetime, one out of every eight adults living in the United States will become either alcoholic or seriously handicapped by alcohol dependency. According to the National Institute on Alcohol Abuse 500,000 Americans a year are classified as alcoholics. Men alcoholics once outnumbered women alcoholics, but women now are closing the gap. Several years ago the National Institute of Mental Health estimated one woman alcoholic to 5.5 men, but now the ratio is as high as 50-50. These are staggering facts and I wonder what this kind of drinking is doing to the home!

The plain fact that drink does play havoc in the home is corroborated by the prophet Habakkuk who wrote, "Yea also, because he transgresseth by wine, *he is* a proud man, neither keepeth at home . . ." (Habakkuk 2:5).

Drink can come between a man and his family. It can take food from the table, shoes from the children's feet, and prosperity from the doors. Mrs. Evangeline Booth put it this way, "Drink has drained more blood, blinded more eyes, twisted more limbs, dethroned more reason and dug more graves than any other poisonous scourge that ever swept its death dealing waves across the world."

When men, especially those who are husbands and fathers, take to drink, the rest of the household lives in fear, trouble and want. A young lady once told me that she had no idea her husband drank when she married him but now he was drinking to excess and had turned to beating her. That home never had a chance; drink had made havoc of it before it ever found happiness.

The man who drinks, or the woman who drinks, is not likely a good provider, and the scripture says, "But if any provide not for his own, and specially for those of his own house, he hath denied the faith, and is worse than an infidel" (I Timothy 5:8). When the necessities of life are withheld because fathers or mothers are drinking, then hell and havoc will rage.

One of the most sordid stories in all of the Bible took place in a home where drink got the upper hand. Lot's two daughters devised a plan saying, "Come, let us make our father drink wine, and we will lie with him, that we may preserve seed of our father" (Genesis 19:32). They proceeded to get their father drunk and later had two sons. The one son became the father of the Moabites, while the other son became the father of the Ammonites. These two nations became the arch enemy of God's people. Here is the evidence. The facts are final. You can't have drink in the house without courting trouble within and enemies without.

The Problem of Divorce

According to the latest statistics, divorce is a growing problem. A nationwide poll in the United States revealed that four out of every ten marriages winds up in divorce. The rate has been rising steadily — as much as 56 percent in a ten-year span. Needless to say, this increase in divorce is playing havoc in the home.

It is extremely difficult to have peace in the home when it is divided. You can't have children living with mother, and father making a monthly visit to take them for a drive, without having unrest. Divorce is against the laws of God and is never a part of His plan. Divorce is a result of hardheartedness, and this always causes trouble.

". . . Moses because of the hardness of your hearts suffered you to put away your wives: but from the beginning it was not so" (Matthew 19:8). How was it in the beginning? ". . . Have ye not read, that he which made *them* at the beginning made them male and female, And said, For this cause shall a man leave father and mother, and shall cleave to his wife: and they twain shall be one flesh? Wherefore they are no more twain, but one flesh. What therefore God hath joined together, let not man put asunder" (Matthew 19:4-6). No wonder the home has been thrown into bedlam, for when men walk contrary to God's laws they fall headlong into disaster.

There is but one substantial ground for divorce, and that is "fornication" which Moffatt and Weymouth translate as "unchastity" and Goodspeed translates as "unfaithfulness." "Whosoever shall put away his wife, except *it be* for fornication, and shall marry another, committeth adultery: and whoso marrieth her which is put away doth commit adultery" (Matthew 19:9). Before you allow yourself the luxury of what Living Letters calls "sex sins," consider seriously the fact that it will probably lead you to the divorce courts and there will be havoc in your home. If you don't think that divorce leads to hell in the home and heart, hear what Acting Judge Morris Ploscowe of New York asks you to consider before seeking divorce:

Loneliness — Divorce may bring new freedom, but it is a freedom to be alone, and most of us are so constituted that we cannot live alone.

Frustration — Divorce leaves a scar. The wound may heal but the scar remains.

Envy — Jealousy can rear its ugly head toward the second wife or the second husband.

Privation — How can you maintain yourself and your children financially? What if the alimony is not enough or won't be paid?

Children — Can you manage them alone? With whom are they to live? What arrangements shall be made for visits? Who gets the children in the case of sickness or remarriage? The poor children are deprived of a proper home and all hope for happiness and harmony is gone.

Residence — It isn't easy to go back and live with mother, and it isn't easy to live alone amid the prying eyes of curious neighbors.

Here are some of the aching issues that make divorce an enemy of home life. Case history after case history proves divorce to be a major tragedy with wide repercussions on mental and physical health as well as on the family unit. Divorce creates no end of trouble and God hates it. "For the Lord, the God of Israel, saith that he hateth putting away . . ." (Malachi 2:16). Take God's way and trust him to save your home from havoc.

God's way is the best way, though I may not see;
Why sorrows and trials oft gather round me.
He ever is seeking my gold to refine;
So humble I'll trust him, my Saviour Divine.
God's way is the best way,
God's way is the right way.
I'll trust him always,
He knoweth the best.

The Problem of Delinquency

When I speak here of delinquency I am not referring specifically to juvenile delinquency. There are, for example, delinquent husbands who fail to love their wives. They abuse them, beat them, and neglect them. One party talked to me by phone and told me that her husband was constantly cursing her and wanted to know what could be done to help the situation. Another young lady wept as she told me how her husband beat her time and again and even after the police had been called he had continued to beat her mercilessly.

The scripture warns against such conduct when it says, "Therefore take heed to your spirit, and let none deal treacherously against the wife of his youth" (Malachi 2:15). Again the Bible admonishes, "Likewise, ye husbands, dwell with them according to knowledge, giving honour unto the wife, as unto the weaker vessel . . ." (I Peter 3:7). A husband who fails to respect his wife does not realize that he is a part of her, and ". . . no man ever yet hated his own flesh . . ." (Ephesians 5:29). If men would do as the Lord asked, "Husbands, love *your* wives, and be not bitter against them" (Colossians 3:19), there would be a great deal more peace in many homes today.

We have some delinquent wives as well. There are those women who fail to respect their husbands, and who are forever nagging them about something until they lose heart. There are some wives who never want to be at home.

The Bible teaches them to be "keepers at home" (Titus 2:5) but they can never content themselves this way. We have the wife who is never satisfied, who has never learned to be content with what she has, and is more set on climbing the social ladder than looking after her home. Today's society is plagued with women who just want to go out to work. They want to make their own money and spend their own money, never content with being dependent upon their good husbands. A few years ago PTA Magazine singled out "permissive parents and working mothers" as serious problems in the home. The scriptures say, ". . . and the wife *see* that she reverence *her* husband" (Ephesians 5:33).

If husbands and wives would quit running around, quit flirting with the opposite sex, and settle down to honest, holy living, harmony might be restored to the modern home. There is no peace when there is no respect for one's partner.

There are delinquent parents who fail to administer proper discipline and neglect their family spiritually or physically. All of these matters bring havoc to the home. Sometimes there is unrest because of delinquent teenagers.

According to Living Letters Paraphrased Epistles one of the signs of the last days is that children will be "Disobedient to their parents, ungrateful to them and thoroughly bad" (II Timothy 3:2). Such children are causing much pain and woe in their homes and need to be warned that "The eye *that* mocketh at *his* father, and despiseth to obey *his* mother, the ravens of the valley shall pick it out, and the young eagles shall eat it" (Proverbs 30:17).

The admonition to all such youth is found in the words of Solomon, "My son, hear the instruction of thy father, and forsake not the law of thy mother" (Proverbs 1:8). Some teens think it is smart to drink, and that it gives them favor with girls. We have teens who feel they can pull the wool over everyone's eyes and smooth talk their way out of any situation. Some figure they can get away with any caper because they have their parents wrapped around their fingers.

Many a mother or father has to nurse an aching or broken heart, and the home is without rest day or night, because teenagers refuse to heed any warnings. They insist on driving highpowered automobiles at reckless speeds and going with girls who have rejected virginity as a virtue. This kind of youngster keeps the home in constant restlessness for fear of what might come next. They say that Sunday School is for kids, church is for squares, and the young people of the church are just not up with the times.

If any young person reading this message falls into this category, let me give you a word from God. "A foolish son *is* a grief to his father, a bitterness to her that bare him" (Proverbs 17:25). "A foolish son is the calamity of his father " (Proverbs 19:13). "He that wasteth *his* father, *and* chaseth away *his* mother, *is* a son that causeth shame, and bringeth reproach. Cease, my son, to hear the instruction *that causeth to* err from the words of knowledge" (Proverbs 19:26,27).

Study the call of the wise Solomon of old before it is too late. Avoid the grief, heartache and reproach some parents have to bear because of the foolishness of their children.

Peace may never reign again in some homes because of the foolishness of a child or the stubbornness of a parent.

But tragedy can be averted by inviting God into your lives, at an old-fashioned altar of prayer.

8

Harmony in the Home

The queen of every happy home is charity. Love lubricates all of life's happy and harmonious relationships, and it is the principal thing, a point the Bible makes very clear. Imagine what harmony we would enjoy in the home if love ruled supreme. Love that was slow to lose patience, that always looked for a way to be constructive, that was not possessive, that had good manners and was not touchy. If love like this was to rule, we would have a veritable heaven on earth. God's word makes it plain that harmony in the home hinges on love.

Husbands, Love Your Wives

Ephesians 5:25-28 emphasizes a point strongly when it says, "Husbands, love your wives, even as Christ also loved the church, and gave himself for it; That he might sanctify and cleanse it with the washing of water by the word, That he might present it to himself a glorious church, not having spot, or wrinkle, or any such thing; but that it should be holy and without blemish. So ought men to love their wives as their own bodies. He that loveth his wife loveth himself."

Love that gives itself speaks of devotion and when we are devoted to our partner it makes for wonderful harmony. It's the devotion of sacrifice that is referred to here. It calls for a loving attitude of concern, compassion and understanding toward the "weaker vessel" — the desire to be helpful and encouraging, and a resolve to make her life happy and worth living. It's the love that goes beyond the realm of words and reaches to the borders of a wife's needs — devotion that will take the husband away from his golf, work or pleasure long enough to take the children off their mother's hands for a while, so that she can get out for a change of pace.

What kind of harmony can you have if the husband always has to come first, and his love toward his wife will not allow him to relinquish any of his selfish pursuits? How would it work if we were to heed the further admonition in Ephesians, Chapter 5, where it says, "Nevertheless let every one of you in particular so love his wife even as himself . . ." (Ephesians 5:33). If you were to follow that instruction you would love your wife enough to let her enjoy some of life's leisure moments in this mad, mad world of ours.

Philips' translation of Colossians 3:19 reads like this, "husbands, be sure you give your wives much love and sympathy: Don't let bitterness and resentment spoil your marriage." Paul is trying to tell you not to be miserable with your wife and not to let a bitter spirit spoil a good relationship. I believe true, loyal love will remedy all resentment. You can have harmony in the home if you are willing to pay the price that is demanded.

Wives, Love Your Husbands

Colossians 3:18 says, "Wives, submit yourselves unto your own husbands, as it is fit in the Lord." It is honoring to the Lord to see a wife showing respect and honor toward her husband, and Paul says, "Teach the young women to be sober, to love their husbands . . . " (Titus 2:4). A woman's love is strong and it never fails to evoke a mutual relationship.

This is illustrated beautifully in the story of John Roebling, Pittsburg's famous bridge builder. After his wife died he wrote the following tribute in the family Bible: "Of those angels in human form who are blessing this earth by their unselfish love and devotion, this dear departed wife was one. She never thought of herself, she only thought of others. No trace of ill will toward any person ever entered her unselfish bosom. And, oh, what a treasure of love she was toward her own children. No faults were ever discovered, she knew only forbearance, patience and kindness." Notice now the reciprocal nature of her love. "My only regret" he says, "that such pure unselfishness was not sufficiently appreciated by myself. In a higher sphere of life I hope to meet you again, dear Johanna, and I also hope that my own love and devotion will then be more deserving of yours."

There seems to be no limit to the power and glory of a woman's love but, what a hell on earth they can make if they do not learn to love their husbands.

What can be more unbearable than a nagging and contentious woman? What can drive a man to drink and to the devil quicker than to live with a brawling woman? Better that a man was never born than to have to endure such a miserable existence. The wise old Solomon stated it well in Proverbs 25:24 which reads *"It is* better to dwell in the corner of the house top, than with a brawling woman and in a wide house." ". . . the contentions of a wife *are* a continual dropping" (Proverbs 19:13), and it's better that you live at peace in one room than to have everything and have to put up with a cantankerous woman. Young woman, love your husband for it is still true that, "A virtuous woman *is* a crown to her husband . . ." (Proverbs 12:4). What a treasure is found when a good wife has been discovered. "Who can find a virtuous woman? for her price *is* far above rubies. The heart of her husband doth safely trust in her . . ." (Proverbs 31:10, 11). A virtuous woman will let her love shine out in the way she keeps herself, the way she speaks to her husband and the way she speaks *of* him.

If you love your husband show it by keeping up your appearance as though you care how you look when he arrives home, and by taking some time to talk with him about his work and his interests. Love like this takes a little effort, but it will bring real harmony into your home life.

Mothers, Love Your Children

Love is something money can't buy. The poorest of mothers can purchase and provide love for their children.

Love is not lavishing good things upon your children. It is not found in the cold atmosphere of conveniences, but is provided in the warmth of patience and understanding. We love our children when we are willing to be "keepers at home" in order to give them the attention they need. Sometimes that attention may be in the form of a kiss or caress and other times it may be in the form of disciplinary correction. It may be to apply a bandage or to open the cookie jar for your child and a few of his dirty-faced friends.

". . . a child left *to himself* bringeth his mother to shame" (Proverbs 29:15). You can't just leave children to find their own way, you have to make yourself available and be around to make sure they are looked after. Social climbers and working women are real contributions toward juvenile delinquency. The Lord asks the pertinent question, "Can a woman forget her sucking child, that she should not have compassion on the son of her womb?" (Isaiah 49:15). Woe unto us if we do not have enough love and compassion to "Train up a child in the way he should go . . ." (Proverbs 22:6).

Children need the security of your corrective love at times too. "Foolishness *is* bound in the heart of a child; *but* the rod of correction shall drive it far from him" (Proverbs 22:15).

Your children will bless you for saving them from their stark foolishness that would otherwise spell their ruin. Your "children (will) arise up, and call her (you) blessed" (Proverbs 31:28), if you have loved them enough to be stern and strict when it was necessary. "Correct thy son, and he shall give thee rest; yea, he shall give delight unto thy soul" (Proverbs 29:17). "Delight unto thy soul" speaks to me of harmony and happiness. You are going to enjoy immense bliss if you truly love your children. Love them enough to give them the security of home and corrective help when you see the need.

A mother's love has brought all of us more memories, more courage, hope, and joy — more mighty men and more happy homes, than any other single thing under heaven.

Here is a little legend that will help us express this matchless miracle of a mother's love: "God sent an angel down from heaven to find the most beautiful thing on earth and bring it back to heaven. When the angel saw the flowers at springtime he said "These must be the most beautiful things on earth," and he gathered them up to take with him back to heaven. Then he met a child of wondrous beauty and golden hair and lovely smile. When he saw the child he said, "This must be the most wondrous thing on earth. Nothing could be sweeter than the smile of that innocent child." Farther along, in a remote valley, he came to a humble cottage where a mother sat in the doorway with her little babe on her lap. As he watched her beautiful and tender care for the little babe, he said, "This must be the fairest thing on earth. I will take the mother's love with me back to heaven." When he reached the portals of heaven the flowers had faded and were dead, the smile on the child's face had changed into a scowl — but the mother's love was unchanged." Just a legend, but what a fact it reveals. Nothing can bring more harmony into a home than a mother's love.

Children, Love Your Parents

"Honour thy father and thy mother" (Exodous 20:12) is the first commandment with promise. The great apostle Paul tells us that we are to obey our parents, "That it may be well with thee, and thou mayest live long on the earth" (Ephesians 6:3).

There is nothing more thrilling than to have obedient and loving children in the home. Any home that is blessed with children who honor and respect their parents is a happy one. What joy to have worry-free nights and fun-filled days with a family that heeds the laws of their mother and obeys the instructions of their father. Proverbs 23:15,16 puts it this way, "My son, if thine heart be wise, my heart shall rejoice, even mine. Yea, my reins shall rejoice, when thy lips speak right things." And verses 24-25: "The father of the righteous shall greatly rejoice: and he that begetteth a wise *child* shall have joy of him. Thy father and thy mother shall be glad, and she that bare thee shall rejoice." What harmony and happiness comes into the home when the children are on the straight and narrow way that leadeth to everlasting life. What feelings and felicity overtake the mother and the father who find their children speaking right things and living righteously in this present wicked age.

Love for our parents will take the drudgery out of the mundane tasks of life. We won't grumble quite so much when we're asked to leave our play to run an errand or, if we're called upon to do some of the work around the house. If you love your parents you'll not want to bring them to shame by your careless, slovenly ways or by taking to drink and other sinful habits that would cause them heartache. You will want to shun the very appearance of evil in order to keep the family from remorse and sadness.

Let me leave you with this admonition, "My son, if sinners entice thee, consent thou not" (Proverbs 1:10). Be a wise child. Love your mom and dad. Help them build a happy home here on earth and establish an unbroken circle around the throne of God. Remember that, "A wise son maketh a glad father" (Proverbs 10:1) and "Whoso keepeth the law *is* a wise son" (Proverbs 28:7). It is well pleasing to God when he can behold a wise and prudent child.

Two verses from Philips translation that are applicable and appropriate are Colossians 3:14,15 which say, "And above everything else be truly loving, for love is the golden chain of all the virtues. Let the harmony of God reign in your hearts, remembering that as members of the same body (or family) you are called to live in harmony, and never forget to be thankful for what God has done for you."

These words belong to each and every member in the home who truly desire to have harmony:

Any Husband or Wife — !

Let us be guests in one another's house
With deferential "no" and courteous "yes";
Let us take care to hide our foolish moods
Behind a certain show of cheerfulness.

Let us avoid all sullen silences;
We should find fresh and sprightly things to say;
I must be fearful lest you find me dull,
And you must dread to bore me anyway.

Let us knock at each other's heart,
Glad of a chance to look within — and yet,
Let us remember that to force one's way
Is the unpardoned breach of etiquette.

So, shall I be host — you, the hostess,
Until all need for entertainment ends;
We shall be lovers when the last door shuts,
But better still — WE SHALL BE FRIENDS.
                              — Carol Haynes

9

Heaven in the Home

It is still true that "the family that prays together stays together." It is so because through prayer we are inviting Heaven to bless this earthly unit. Heaven's blessings can only be enjoyed in our home as we make a place for the sanctifying presence of the Holy Spirit. He hath been sent forth to sweeten all of life's relationships.

Why do so few homes enjoy true heavenly happiness? J. Edgar Hoover of the FBI best answers this question when he says, "If there is to be peace and happiness in our homes, then we as a nation must turn to God and to the practice of daily family altars." The poet put it this way:

"That house shall be preserved, and never shall decay;
Where God and Christ are worshipped, day by day."

A Daily Family Altar

The home where Heaven is honored "never shall decay." God could say of Abraham, "For I know him, that he will command his children and his household after him, and they shall keep the way of the Lord, to do justice and judgment; that the Lord may bring upon Abraham that which he hath spoken of him" (Genesis 18:19). Abraham was to have all that Heaven ever promised for any home because he led his children in the ways of the Lord.

Here is a heritage anyone can give their children. You do not have to be rich, influential or popular to see that the windows of Heaven are opened upon your home. It's mostly a matter of decision and determination as you take your stand with men like Joshua saying, ". . . as for me and my house, we will serve the Lord" (Joshua 24:15). Another strong affirmation of scripture is found in Psalm 101:2 where it states, ". . . I will walk within my house with a perfect heart."

It's no small task to erect and maintain a family altar in the hectic days that are upon us, but you could be sorry if you don't. Eli, a priest of God, failed in this function and the Bible tells us, "the sons of Eli *were* sons of Belial; (or sons of the devil) they knew not the Lord" (I Samuel 2:12). God told Eli how this all happened when he said, ". . . his sons made themselves vile, and he restrained them not" (I Samuel 3:13). When you are too busy or too preoccupied to show any interest in the family altar then you are just too busy.

A returned missionary, shocked at the conditions in America, noted the fall of the family altar as one of the chief changes in American life: "My father gathered his family together each morning," he stated, "and commended us to God's keeping before we separated for the duties of the day. On my return from India I found that he had given up the practice of family prayer entirely and that my younger brothers and sisters were individualists who cared nothing for the moral and religious influence of the home. What is true of my father's home is true of many homes throughout the length and breadth of the land. The home is no longer a unit; family life, with its spiritual and moral training is very largely a thing of the past. This in my judgment is the explanation of the lack of moral earnestness and disregard for the rights of others so strikingly apparent." If we neglect the place of family prayer we're going to live to regret it, and to mourn our failure with bitter tears. We must not throw aside this God-given responsibility.

J. Edgar Hoover spoke out on this matter on another occasion and said, "More children are being sacrificed from the altar of indifference as parents throw aside responsibility."

We are totally responsible for establishing a pattern and setting an example. What our children do and how much of Heaven we have in our home largely depends upon our leadership. The Bible says this of a wicked king: "And he did evil in the sight of the Lord, and walked in the way of his father, and in the way of his mother . . . who made Israel to sin" (I Kings 22:52). It says of a good king, he "did *that which was* right in the eyes of the Lord, as did . . . his father" (I Kings 15:11).

St. Paul made it plain when he wrote, "Fathers . . . bring them (your children) up in the nurture and admonition of the Lord" (Ephesians 6:4). It seems obvious that it is the duty of fathers to train their children in spiritual matters.

Dr. G. Campbell Morgan points up the importance of a good example in this matter when he says, "If you neglect prayer, and if the family altar is a thing you can lightly lay aside, your boy will never erect it in his own home presently."

When it comes to bringing Heaven down into the home and into the life of our family there is just no substitute for the family altar. Bishop Palmer of the Methodist church said, "It has been my privilege to study in some of the greatest universities in the world and to sit at the feet of some of the wisest men on earth. But altogether this does not compare with what has been given me in family worship. Without this heritage it is highly doubtful if I would be in the church today, to say nothing of being in the service of the church."

This is where Heaven can come down upon the home — at an altar where every member participates in Bible reading and prayer. A minister friend once told me of going into the home of one of his parishioners only to find them all upon their knees seeking God. Prayer time at the family altar had brought the blessings of Heaven down into the home, and into each heart, and all were engaged in fervent supplication before the Lord. The young boy of the home was receiving the Baptism of the Holy Spirit and was speaking in other tongues as the Spirit gave him utterance. (Acts 2:4.) The entire family were rejoicing in the presence of God. It brings to mind a similar result in the book of Acts. Cornelius was, the Bible says, "A devout *man,* and one that feared God with all his house . . ." (Acts 10:2). God saw this man's heart and sent Peter to his house and as he preached to his family we read "the Holy Ghost fell on all them which heard the word" (Acts 10:44), "For they heard them speak with tongues, and magnify God" (Acts 10:46).

Your Spiritual Attitude

To have heaven's influence in your home you must have a wholesome attitude toward God-ordained mediums of manifestation. You've got to have a spiritual approach to God's plan.

Ask yourself this question. "What is my attitude toward the house of God?" When it comes time to attend the house of God, do you look for a thousand reasons why it would be impossible to make it, or do you say with the psalmist, "I was glad when they said unto me, Let us go into the house of the Lord" (Psalm 122:1). Do you really love the house of God? Do you look forward to attending all services, when possible, and are you willing servants in the house of God? Does your love for God's house ever reach the heights it takes to say, ". . . I had rather be a doorkeeper in the house of my God, than to dwell in the tents of wickedness" (Psalm 84:10). "A day in thy courts *is* better than a thousand" (Psalm 84:10), was the psalmist's way of expressing his joy in God's house.

A spiritual and heavenly atmosphere in the home can only be nurtured by a wholesome attitude toward all of your church's spiritual activities. If you order your children off to the youth service in mid-week then you should be equally enthusiastic about getting yourself out to the mid-week prayer service. If we are to raise Christian workers we must be workers ourselves.

Hebrews 10:25 puts it like this, "Not forsaking the assembling of ourselves together, as the manner of some *is*; but exhorting *one another:* and so much the more, as ye see the day approaching."

"The assembling of ourselves together" is what the Bible is contending for and this is precisely what it takes to create a spiritual tone in the home. Go to Sunday School together, sit in the family pew together and attend the great Sunday evening evangelistic service together. If you have the bad habit of neglecting your local church then you can be sure that it is going to affect the spiritual atmosphere in your home.

I will praise God forever for the attitude of my parents toward the local church. Our home was opened every month for a men's bible class to come and sing the songs of Zion, offer prayer and give testimony to their faith. This brought a little more of Heaven into our home. I can remember listening from my upstairs bedroom as their voices would swell with the melodies of the church and with words of testimony. This type of activity helped bring blessings to the entire family.

Ask yourself one further question. "What is my attitude toward the Lord's day?" Is the Lord's day a joy, a drudge, or just another day for play? How you treat the Lord's day can have a great influence for good or evil in your home. Isaiah 56:2 says, "Blessed (or happy) *is* the man *that* doeth this, and the son of man that *layeth* hold on it; that keepeth the sabbath from polluting it, and keepeth his hand from doing any evil."

It's a happy man who has learned to respect the sabbath, and has taught his family the same divine principle. Hear what it says in Isaiah 58:13 and 14, "If thou turn away thy foot from the sabbath, *from* doing thy pleasure on my holy day; and call the sabbath a delight, the holy of the Lord, honourable; and shalt honour him, not doing thine own ways, nor finding thine own pleasure, nor speaking *thine own* words: Then shalt thou delight thyself in the Lord; and I will cause thee to ride upon the high places of the earth, and feed thee with the heritage of Jacob thy father: for the mouth of the Lord hath spoken *it.*" We are going to ride upon the high places and our family will enjoy feeding upon the great spiritual heritage of our God.

So many people feel that Sunday is the only day they have to get out on the golf course, or to go and visit Aunt Mary, or to get away from life's burdens, but remember, what you sow is exactly what you will reap. "Thy pleasure", "Thine own ways", "Thine own words", and again "Thine own pleasure" must all come second if you want your spirit refreshed and your family enriched. It's no great wonder to me that there is havoc and strife today when men and women can't even find one day in seven for God. All he is asking for is fifty-two days out of a whole year and for those days he has promised us all spiritual blessings in return. If the spiritual tide in your home is low then why not take inventory and find out how you have been spending your Sundays over the past few years.

One last question you should ask yourself. "What is my attitude toward the Word of God and the place of private prayer?" If you lack the sweet presence of God in your own personal life it is much more difficult for you to help lead your family into a spiritual experience. Do you have any place in your daily life for Bible reading and meditation? Do you search the scriptures daily? Do you have any appetite for the Word of the Lord?

Peter wrote in his epistle, ". . . desire (or get an appetite for) the sincere milk of the word, that ye may grow thereby" (I Peter 2:2). "Blessed *is* the man that walketh not in the counsel of the ungodly . . . But his delight *is* in the law of the Lord; and in his law doth he meditate day and night" (Psalm

1:1,2).

It's not too often that you see a mother and father who love the Word of God and find time to pray every day, having troublous times with their family. Heaven pervades the atmosphere of the home where parents are walking in the Spirit and not fulfilling the lusts of the flesh. We need more men at the head of the house leading forth in spiritual matters as Eisenhower did when he led the neighboring nation. He took his oath with the Bible opened at one favorite quotation, Psalm 127:1, which reads: "Except the Lord build the house, they labour in vain that build it: except the Lord keep the city, the watchman waketh *but* in vain."

Do you have that kind of confidence in the Lord and in his Word? Do you really believe that your house will only have heaven's blessings as you look to the Lord, and your children will only be kept as you trust them into his hands? If so, learn the secret of the poet who wrote:

I met God in the morning
When the day was at its best,
And His presence came like sunrise,
Like a glory in my breast.

All day long the Presence lingered,
All day long He stayed with me,
And I sailed in perfect calmness
O'er a very troubled sea.

Other ships were blown and battered,
Other ships were sore distressed,
But the winds that seemed to drive them,
Brought to us a peace and rest.

Then I thought of other mornings,
With a keen remorse of mind,
When I too had loosed the moorings,
With the Presence left behind.

So, I think I know the secret,
Learned from many a troubled way;
You must seek Him in the morning
If you want Him through the day!

Dedicate yourself and your home to God. Believe him —
for a fresh touch of Heaven in your home.

10

No Ordinary Child

What mother views her newborn babe as just an ordinary child? Really now, isn't your infant the most beautiful, the most contented, and the most loving little one you have ever seen?

In reality there has only been one perfect child ever born of woman. The reason is obvious to all who believe in miracles. Jesus was conceived of the Holy Spirit. "Now the birth of Jesus Christ was on this wise: When as his mother Mary was espoused to Joseph, before they came together, she was found with child of the Holy Ghost" (Matthew 1:18). It never happened before and it will never occur again.

Jesus proved to the whole world that he was no ordinary child, when at twelve years of age he confounded all the religious leaders in the temple. In the power of the Spirit, and by faith in his Father he continued to confound all his enemies, even the devil himself, by destroying his works. We should thank God for this example of what He can do with a solitary life that is moved, molded and motivated by the power of the Spirit.

I believe it's possible for parents to make the difference

between an ordinary and an extraordinary child. Mary and Joseph, by faith, followed all of God's directions that led to the birth and growth of the perfect child.

Moses' parents got the same result when, by faith, believing him to be "no ordinary child," they kept him from the destruction of an evil king. It all led to his final choice of following the will of the Lord and to works of greatness for God.

The faith, obedience and love of parents can still lead children into the power of the Spirit, and God will bless them in such a way that everyone will recognize them as "no ordinary child." It will be evident that your children "now are holy" (I Corinthians 7:14). They are separated unto God and, in a very real sense, our children belong to Him.

Dr. Howard C. Estep of World Prophetic Ministry stated it clearly in his booklet on *Family Religion.* The family, or the home, is the world's oldest institution, established long before the church. Even before the Jewish way or worship was brought into being, God established the home and "family religion."

Family religion is defined this way: First of all, a family is a closely-knit group of people who are congretated together through the marriage bond — father, mother and children. Secondly, religion is any particular system in which a systematic search for the ideal life is being embodied and pursued. Family religion is the religious practice by a family interwoven together in a bond of love because of the marriage relationship with all of them seeking, endeavoring and working together to find the ideal way of life.

Noah took his stand for righteousness and his family supported him. Genesis 7:1 says, "And the Lord said unto Noah, Come thou and all thy house into the ark . . ." and Genesis 7:7 tells us, "And Noah went in, and his sons, and his wife, and his sons' wives with him, into the ark." The Lord knows how to deliver our souls and our family from wickedness and the temptation of corruption. "If God spared not the old world, but saved Noah . . . The Lord knoweth how to deliver the godly out of temptations . . ." (II Peter 2:4-9).

Noah taught his family to worship. When he and his family first left the ark after the flood, Noah "builded an altar unto the Lord" (Genesis 8:20). We read the results of this in Genesis 9:1, "And God blessed Noah (*and his sons*)."

Dr. Estep said, "We have drifted away from the spirit of religion in our families. We desperately need to get back to the fundamental principles of the family being together, worshiping together, and living a life for God together."

A real estate agent was trying to sell a woman a house, and she was overheard to say, "A house! What do I need with a house? I was born in a hospital, educated in college, courted in an automobile, and married in a church. I live out of the delicatessen, tin cans and paper bags, I spend my mornings on the golf course, my afternoons at a cocktail party, and my evenings at a nightclub. When I die, I'm going to have my funeral at a mortuary and be buried in a cemetery. What do I need with a house?"

A house may not be necessary to some people, but a home is. It is the fundamental basis of religion, and when American homes began to break down morally, then America began to "come apart at the seams." Today America is tottering morally because she does not have the strong undergirding of religion that includes the whole family.

Let's look briefly at religion. It should definitely be a family affair. Oftentimes we hear a husband say, "Well, my wife is the church member in our family. She takes care of all our religious activities." This should not be so. This is not the way God wants the home to be. Many times we hear parents say, "We take our children to Sunday School." Yes, they take them, deposit them at the entrance, then go away and return in an hour or so to pick them up. Well, if Sunday School is good for the children, why isn't it good for father and mother?

The world *needs* a religion for the entire family. Parents

as well as children need indoctrination of this kind so that as a people we might possess the qualities that make noble, God-fearing characters out of individual people. The very best thing you can do for your children is to make sure they have had the Word of God presented to them by your own example; a standard that you, as a parent, have set in the home.

The peace and prosperity of the human race centers around the home. Wherever there is a community made up of happy homes, we find a happy, contented community. One historical figure stands out, as we take a look into the distant past for the answer to the outstanding family.

The record says, simply, "But Noah found grace in the eyes of the Lord" (Genesis 6:8). God favored this man and all his family in the midst of one of the blackest and bleakest of times. He just refused to be influenced by the corruption prevalent in his society. We are told, ". . . Noah was a just man *and* . . . Noah walked with God" (Genesis 6:9).

The ordinary family in Noah's time, according to the words of Jesus, were eating, drinking and breaking their marriage vows. (Matthew 24:38). The description of the existing degradation would shock any sensible person and put a scare into any sensitive parent. There was very little influence of the Holy Spirit evident amongst men at that time. God almighty was deeply grieved at the way people were living. In Genesis 6:5,6 we read, "And God saw that the wickedness of man *was* great in the earth, and *that* every imagination of the thoughts of his heart *was* only evil continually. And it repented the Lord that he had made man on the earth, and it grieved him at his heart," and again, in Verse 11, "The earth also was corrupt before God, and the earth was filled with violence." The situation had deteriorated until God had to take drastic action. Genesis 6:13 reads, "And God said unto Noah, The end of all flesh is come before me; for the earth is filled with violence through them; and, behold, I will destroy them with the earth."

We must learn to look upon sin in our children, upon the spirit of the world or conformity to it, as at utter variance with a child which the Holy God has set apart for holiness. The first need of a parent, whose children belong to God, is His personal heritage. Nothing but a life in the holiness of God, a life entirely under the leading of the Holy Spirit, can fit us for watching over and training the children God has given us.

God said of Abraham in Genesis 18:19, "For I know him, that he will command his children and his household after him, and they shall keep the way of the Lord, to do justice and judgment; that the Lord may bring upon Abraham that which he hath spoken of him."

"Noah walked with God." His family saw his life! They saw his obedience to God! (Genesis 6:22.) He obeyed God's voice and his family followed his example!

The Christian family cannot depend on the church alone to provide their children with a Christian education. This training must come from the home as the primary agent of spiritual teaching. In the home, children should learn respect for the leaders of the church. It has been noted that when a pastor is called upon to help a wayward son or daughter, they cannot do so effectively because their position has been undermined and eroded by things the young people heard at home. The real losers in any church problem are the children. Parents can and do make the difference.

The bottom line on this man Noah, who refused to allow himself or his family to follow the prevailing world life-style, is in Hebrews 11:7, "By faith Noah, being warned of God of things not seen as yet, moved with fear, prepared an ark to the saving of his house; by the which he condemned the world, and became heir of the righteousness which is by faith."

Family worship produces high and holy inspiration in the lives of children. They know there is a difference and they learn to experience the blessings of God for themselves. Every young person who has experienced the reality of God's presence in his family realizes there is a definite difference. These boys and girls are fully aware that they are God's property, to be useful in this world as God directs, to be trained with the one purpose of doing God's will and showing forth his glory.

Samson, for example, was a young man raised in an atmosphere of holiness who had some powerful moments when the Spirit of the Lord moved upon his life. He knew the difference between the ordinary, weak ways of this world and the way of strength in the Spirit. He knew what would result if he lost his spiritual strength. He said, "then shall I be weak, and be as another man" (Judges 16:7).

Who wants to be weak and just another man in the crowd? Anyone who takes up the ordinary lifestyle after knowing the way of the Lord always lives to regret it.

Terry Bradshaw of the Pittsburgh Steelers recently testified to this in *Sports Illustrated.* In 1974 his troubles began anew. He was divorced from his wife of eighteen months, Melissa Babish, Miss Teenage America of 1969, and in training camp he lost his starting job to third-year man, Joe Gilliam. If an athlete's career is life in capsule — youth, middle age, old age, all in a dozen years — then Bradshaw suffered a mid-life crisis at 26.

"I'm a Baptist, a Christian," he says. "I pulled away from it in that year. I felt a lot of guilt over the divorce, and I'd lost my job. I'd failed. I didn't become an alcoholic or a whoremonger, but I was moody and depressed and I drank and hustled women in bars — a total jerk having a ball. I have never enjoyed those things. I'd been a devout Christian for so long, getting away from it affected me mentally. The ton of guilt brought me to my knees. I guess you could say that God blitzed me and gave me a shot to the head, and no one threw a flag.' "

Like Samson, Terry Bradshaw didn't take long to realize he wanted something more than to simply be "another man" in the crowd following the weak ways of the world.

So often parents accept the philosophy of this world that "every kid has to have his fling." This is not true, and if you believe it is, then expect to experience the worst. Parents can and do make the difference in the future of their children. The answer is to acknowledge the holiness of God in your children, and in a spiritual environment, believe that you see the Lord's work in their lives. It is the work of the Christian parent to train his children in such dispositions and habits, such ways of thinking and feeling and acting, as shall be in harmony with the faith that they belong to the Holy Spirit dwelling in them and using them as His temple.

History has proven this powerful principle. Look at what Hebrews 11:23-29 tells us of Moses . . . "By faith Moses, when he was born, was hid three months of his parents, because they saw *he was* a proper child; and they were not afraid of the king's commandment (that all babies be put to death)." Look at his great future. He "refused to be called the son of Pharaoh's daughter; Choosing rather to suffer affliction with the people of God . . . he forsook Egypt . . . Esteeming the reproach of Christ greater riches than the treasures in Egypt." He went on to lead the children of Israel out of Egypt and across the Red Sea" as by dry *land.*"

It has been said of John Milton that he was "a tremendous lover of the Bible" and that he "drew the whole of his inspiration from the Bible." During the most impressionable years of his life, his character was molded by his parents. His father had two great passions — passion for the Bible and passion for music! Every evening, when the day's work was done, the family would gather to read and discuss some passage of scripture and would join in singing several of the Psalms. No wonder Milton had such a high regard for the things of God when this love and concern had been cultivated in him from his earliest years.

Let us look at Abraham Lincoln. His mother died when he was just nine years of age. Many times, when he was asked how he had the courage to resist some temptation, he said he never forgot his mother's teaching. All through his life he treasured her last words. She said, "I am going away from you, Abraham, and shall not return. I know that you will be a good boy, and that you will be kind to your father. I want you to live as I have taught you, to love your Heavenly Father and keep His commandments."

Again I say, parents can and do make the difference in the future of their children.

11

Parental Respect: The Fifth Commandment

The beginning of respect or disrespect for all authority has its roots in this commandment: "Honour thy father and thy mother" (Exodous 20:12).

If we will not subject ourselves to parental authority, nor have due respect for it, we are likely to find it hard to subject ourselves to legal authority. If we cannot honor and respect our parents, how can we learn to honor and respect our teachers, our policemen, our minister, or any other man or woman called to help us find our way in life?

Newton says, "You show me a boy or girl who is not a good son or daughter, who does not honour father and mother, and I'll show you one who will not make a good man or woman."

It is important to begin life right! Begin at home! One man put it this way, "Parental authority is the grand, divinely-appointed educator for citizenship. Loyalty to parental law prepares the way to loyalty to civic law." If we can't show any loyal obligation to our parents whom God has given us, how will we be able to show loyal obligation toward God Himself?

Let us see three things in this commandment: first the parent's part; second, the child's part, and then, God's part.

Parents Must Inspire Honor in the Child

If the words "give honor where honor is due" carry any weight at all, then it is certainly laden with meaning here. Ephesians 6:4 says, ". . . fathers, provoke not your children to wrath: but bring them up in the nurture and admonition of the Lord." If we do not conduct our lives honorably and fail in giving our children reason to respect us, they are going to become angry and discouraged. *After they become angry, and fed up with the way we have been leading them, they are going to riot and become delinquent.*

Failure of parents is going to lead to lack of respect if it hasn't already done so. In Numbers we read, "But as for you, your carcases, they shall fall in this wilderness. And your children shall wander in the wilderness forty years, and bear your whoredoms, until your carcases be wasted in the wilderness" (Numbers 14:32,33).

C. M. Ward comments, "That's a long time to get sand in your shoes, and with every step to remember that it was dad's stubbornness and unbelief that were to blame." Fathers and mothers for those forty years of exile weren't worthy of the respect of their sons and daughters.

We owe our children something. First, we owe them *love.* Titus 2:4 says, ". . . teach the young women to . . . love their children." We must love our children, love them with geniune affection because they feel, deeply, any pretense. Children today miss the kind of love they need simply because mother is out to work; talk of divorce and disloyalty keep the home in constant upheaval, and father is too interested in the local pub or club to stay at home. Love is something a child feels when he sees mom baking a batch of cookies for him or when he finds clean clothes and covers awaiting him. The Bible says that loving mothers are "keepers at home" (Titus 2:5). Love is something a child senses when he sees he is provided for, and sees mother and dad are agreeing on domestic needs.

First Timothy 5:8 says, "But if any provide not for his own, and specially for those of his own house, he hath denied the faith, and is worse than an infidel." Children need a sense of security that must come from their parents, those who look after them, and provide for their needs. Love is felt by a child when he is considered a part of the family in all its plans. He feels insecure if he is always left with a baby-sitter. He feels disturbed when he is never taken along because he is considered a bother and a nuisance. We owe our children love!

Secondly, we owe them *authority*. God, in speaking of Abraham, said, ". . . I know him, that he will command his children and his household after him" (Genesis 18:19). Children want to be cared for. They want to feel someone cares enough to lay down a restrictive law of authority. They need to be told about the lack of A's on the report card, or that eleven o'clock is the curfew hour, or that they are to be in Sunday School and church, and no maybe's about any of it.

One journalist stated in Reader's Digest, "Teenagers are often relieved when their parents say, No! Although they put up a big show of wanting more freedom, they are comfortable in the knowledge that strong, supportive arms surround them. They want protection against their own impulsiveness and foolishness."

One woman tells how her daughter came to her as a high school freshman and put up a well-rehearsed plea to fly to a university dance. The answer was a flat "No! You're not ready for such a thing." Her daughter's answer was, "I don't think so either, but I just thought I'd try."

She was relieved when due authority was exerted for her own good by a mother who cared.

Indulgence with a child, when authority is needed, is a curse to them and to the parent. Lack of authority is the reason why our children are rebelling today. They want to be told what is right and what is wrong, and they expect it from their parents. They want to be told about the facts of life from the proper authority. They expect this too from their parents. We owe our children authority!

Thirdly, we owe our children *discipline* or *chastening.* Proverbs 29:15 says, "The rod and reproof give wisdom: but a child left *to himself* bringeth his mother to shame." When your child gets out of line, you owe it to him to chasten him, in love, not in anger, that he might not be left to himself. Children should not be allowed to do as they please. If they do, they ought to be disciplined accordingly. They'll grow up to shame you if you don't restrain them when necessary.

It says of Eli, ". . . I will judge his house for ever for the iniquity which he knoweth; because his sons made themselves vile, and he restrained them not" (I Samuel 3:13). Eli failed to discipline his boys and we read of them that they "*were* sons of Belial (the devil); they knew not the Lord" (I Samuel 2:12) "Wherefore the sin of the young men was very great before the Lord" (I Samuel 2:17).

If you want your children to lose respect for you — if you want to see them go to hell — then just leave them to themselves. Proverbs 23:13,14 tells us, "Withhold not correction from the child: for *if* thou beatest him with the rod, he shall not die. Thou shalt beat him with the rod, and shalt deliver his soul from hell." And again in Proverbs 13:24, "He that spareth his rod hateth his son: but he that loveth him chasteneth him betimes."

Children Must Carry Honor For Their Parents

"Honour thy father and thy mother." Love and respect for parents is something we must carry through life with us. When we become mature, we must never forget the parental goodness we have enjoyed. Colossians 3:20 says, "Children, obey *your* parents in all things: for this is well pleasing unto the Lord." The child who respects and honors his parents, pleases the Lord. It is shown through our obedience. Obedience is something we render, not because we know we'll be punished if we are disobedient, but because we love our parents and we want to do the will of God.

One mother commanded her children with a rope held up before them. They obeyed. They did not honor their mother. They honored the rope!

What we need to realize is that God is displeased and dishonored when children show disrespect for their parents. A commandment of God is broken when a child is allowed to talk back to his parents. (They are not the "old lady" and the "old man." They are parents, and they must be honored.)

There are two types of obedience. One is *ready obedience.* "Children, obey your parents in the Lord: for this is right" (Ephesians 6:1). It is right to obey your parents without asking questions. You should hearken to their counsel, subscribe to their commandments, and pay attention to what is expected of you. If your parents say, No to the dance, or if they say you must follow their plans, or that you must perform certain duties, then, out of honor and respect you must show ready obedience.

Let me illustrate from a personal experience. When I was eighteen, my parents were moving from Galt to Ottawa, and I had a good job and did not want to move with them. My dad, in concern for my salvation, said, "You're going with us."

Now at my age I could have said, "I'm not going," and walked out right there and then. My father did not threaten me in any way, but I respected him, so I quit my job and went with them. You can call that ready obedience. It was obedience that resulted from the honor my parents had established in me. Ready obedience, which results from reverential respect, will keep you from evil.

There is *absent obedience.* Absent obedience is the real test of how much children really honor and respect their parents. When they are taught to shun certain evils, asked not to frequent certain places, or to break off with certain company, then the test will come in absent obedience.

Children owe it to their parents to obey them, not only when the parents are around, but also when they are not around. How often a young person, not wanting to bring reproach on his parents, has refrained from conscious evil, such as smoking, drinking or fornication. When we see a child, while away from home, acting just as he would if his parents were near at hand, we can't help but know that he honors and respects them.

There is the story of a boy who, being invited to go to the circus, declined to go saying, "Father don't approve of them."

His friend further enticed him saying, "I'd go just once if I were you Johnny."

"I shan't do it," said the boy.

"Why not?"

" 'Cause," said Johnny, "I couldn't look my father in the eye right, and I can now."

There is no finer answer to enticement, no answer so admirable, than, "My parents do not approve." Proverbs 13:1 says "A wise son heareth his father's instruction . . ." And in Proverbs 15:5 we read ". . . he that regardeth reproof is prudent." "A wise son maketh a glad father . . ." (Proverbs 10:1). There is nothing so pleasant to a parent than to know his son or daughter has proven to be upright when tested. It is also the child's reward. One great man said after winning a battle, "My chief pleasure is, that my parents will hear of my victory."

There is *affectionate obedience.* Affectionate obedience will cause children to obey their parents because they love them. This story is told of George Washington. He had set his heart on entering the navy and going to sea, and his mother had yielded a reluctant consent. As he was ready to leave home, he went to say good-bye to his mother. He found her in tears. That was enough for him. He turned to his servant and said, "Take my trunk back again to my room. I will not break my mother's heart to please myself." This is what I call honoring one's parents! Breaking off from doing what pleases us to keep from breaking their hearts!

The Hon. Thomas H. Benton, when speaking to a ladies' group in New York, once commented, "My mother asked me never to use tobacco, and I have never touched it from that day to this. She asked me never to gamble, and I have never learned to gamble. When I was seven years old she asked me not to drink. I made a resolution of total abstinence. That resolution I have never broken. And now, whatever service I have been able to render to my country, or whatever honor I may have gained, I owe it to my mother."

That is honoring your mother — when you obey her because you love her and then speak highly of her to others!

It was the affection of Jesus that led him to make a provision for his mother when he was about to leave the scene. He so honored His mother, that He set before us a beautiful example. "Then saith he to the disciple, Behold thy mother! And from that hour that disciple took her unto his own home." (John 19:27).

John Edward said in his diary, when only twenty years of age, "I now plainly perceive what great obligations I am under to love and honour my parents. I have great reason to believe that their counsel and education have been my making; notwithstanding at the time it seemed to do me so little good."

Promise of Prosperity To Result From Honor Given

"That thy days may be long upon the land which the Lord thy God giveth thee" (Exodus 20:12). There is a promised blessing for all those who honor their parents. Paul says this is the first commandment with promise. The man who follows this law is likely to follow all the other laws that lead a man to be blessed with health and prosperity. If you want to be a top graduate from this school of life begin by honoring your parents. "Obey your parents that it may be well with you."

Of course, the opposite is true of those who disobey their

parents. Deuteronomy 27:16 says, "Cursed be he that setteth light by his father or his mother." Also in Proverbs 30:17 "The eye *that* mocketh at *his* father, and despiseth to obey *his* mother, the ravens of the valley shall pick it out, and the young eagles shall eat it."

Proverbs 3:1-4,7,8 says, "My son, forget not my law; but let thine heart keep my commandments: For length of days, and long life, and peace, shall they add to thee. Let not mercy and truth forsake thee: bind them about thy neck; write them upon the table of thine heart: So shalt thou find favour and good understanding in the sight of God and man. Be not wise in thine own eyes: fear the Lord, and depart from evil. It shall be health to thy navel, and marrow to thy bones."

The blessing of almighty God is present on those who will keep this and all other commandments.

12

Suffering, Sickness and Sacrifice

My own family history reveals something of the symphony of suffering and much of the glory of God's dealings with men. When Jesus Christ enters the scene of any life or home, the script is rewritten. This is precisely what happened in our household.

In the full flow of a prosperous life, my father's body came under the assualt of tuberculosis. The year was 1938 and wonder drugs and miracle cures were unavailable to the medical profession. Internal hemorrhaging caused my father to choke on his own blood and the doctors informed my mother that the situation was so critical that Dad would probably survive for only a matter of months.

Feeling the full impact of this heartbreaking situation, my mother was able to recover sufficiently to prepare herself to go out and earn a living for the family. She knew she had to be strong for the sake of the children. Joyce, Bob and I were all under the age of eight. Many times the burden seemed too much to bear, but she always found the courage to keep going. This critical hour in her life seemed an opportune time for God to work. "God works in mysterious ways His wonders to perform" worked!

A Christian lady, who lived across the street from us, saw our need and had compassion for our suffering. She immediately began to pray for us and also asked others to pray. Thank God for Christian neighbors who put their faith into action. She invited Mother to a service at her church, and this proved to be a turning point in Mom's life. It inevitably affected the lives of the entire family.

Mother had a positive encounter with Christ, found the great Burden-Bearer, and began to live a purposeful life. She understood now what Jesus meant when He said, "Come unto me, all ye that labour and are heavy laden, and I will give you rest. . . . For my yoke is easy, and my burden is light" (Matthew 11:28,30).

Arriving home at Father's bedside, she told of her Christian commitment, her forgiven sins, and how the joy of the Lord had brought peace to her heart. My father was very unsympathetic, to say the least, and suggested that this might be all right for her, but that he didn't want any part of religion. Inside, I think he felt hurt and jealous because she had a new peace and a Presence in her life that he couldn't share.

However, Mother was determined to live for God and she began to take her three children to church and Sunday School. Thank God for a mother with a holy boldness and a desire to be in church and Sunday School *with* her children, rather than just sending them on their own.

Now that transformation had begun in our home, nothing was going to stop it. God performed one miracle after another. My older sister Joyce followed in the Master's steps in her earliest years, and set a good example for my brother Bob and me.

My father's encounter with Christ came on a Sunday morning while lying alone in bed, listening to the radio ministry of "America Back to God." Suddenly, he found himself weeping tears of repentance as all resistance toward God vanished in a new surge of love and faith. When Mother returned home, she was alarmed at Father's tears and asked what was wrong with him. He replied, "The same thing that's wrong with you!" All those faithful prayers had finally ripened to overflowing joy.

This was just the beginning of our new life! From that point on God was able to gain access to our home in a much more complete way. The pastor and many godly people from the local church were able to bring inspiration to my father on his bed of sickness, making our home into a haven of rest and hope. The men's group of the church visited my father on a regular basis, and the beautiful moments of Christian fellowship left a lasting effect upon each member of the family. In later years, these experiences and impressions brought great blessing to my own life and ministry. There is nothing to compare with the inspiration of a godly home, as bad habits are gradually replaced with good promises from the Bible.

Even though my father was now a follower of Jesus Christ, he was still a very sick man, and was to spend ten years in bed with tuberculosis. Economically, our lives were still very unstable, but now my parents were able to pray for food, fuel and funds; not once, but many times through the years.

I vividly recall a time when we were faced with the necessity of raising a substantial sum of money demanded by the insurance company. There were prayers and tears offered freely to our Heavenly Father and the answer was miraculous. As is the case with many answers to prayer, the funds were already in the house, in this case being saved for a rare vacation. The decision was made to take these precious savings to pay the debt. The men's group, knowing nothing of our situation, decided amongst themselves to present my father with a gift of money so that the Shrier's could have a holiday. The amount they raised was precisely the same as that which had been spent to meet the demands of the insurance company. Isn't God good!

From this point on, our provision was often supplied by outside sources. Money arrived in the mail from private parties who felt constrained to help us, knowing nothing of our plight. And of course, Joyce and Bob and I contributed everything we could earn in part-time jobs like selling papers, to supplement our family income.

As time went by, there were major decisions to be made about my father's medical treatment which could never have been determined apart from prayer and complete trust in the promises of God. Certainly one of life's greatest decisions came when Father was faced with the alternative of a prolonged sickness with a premature death, or submitting to surgery in order to have a longer life with his family. The latter seemed to be the obvious choice, although the doctors gave him only a 50 percent chance of surviving the operation.

After considerable deliberation and divine guidance through prayer and meditation, Father chose to have the operation which would collapse his left lung. He went to hospital, God's people went to prayer, and God answered swiftly and supernaturally. He guided the physicians, then stepped into the scene Himself to demonstrate His own healing power, thus surpassing all that had been done up to this point.

This became a documented miracle of physical healing. Not only did subsequent X-rays reveal an astonishing removal of tuberculosis from the body, but to this day, Dad suffers no discomfort or deformity from the collapsed lung or the ribs which were removed. You can feel his chest, and you will be certain that he has as normal a rib cage and straight posture as any healthy twenty-year-old.

God gave Dad back his strength, his health and his vitality for life, after ten trying years in bed. His first job after all these years was a managerial one, and along with that came many new opportunities to serve God in His great Kingdom. He became active with a local Christian Business Men's group, Child Evangelism Fellowship, and church activities, all of which led him to more and more opportunities to share his personal testimony.

Today, at seventy years of age, he is deeply involved, as he has been for the last twenty-seven years, as a lay-evangelist with the Christian and Missionary Alliance churches. He has ministered in countries including Africa, Equador, South America and the United States, as well as extensively in Canada. This year he made his third trip to Africa, speaking to native ministers and crusade audiences. The title of his autobiography is an appropriate summation: "I Don't Know What Your God Can Do, But *My God Can Do Anything!*"*

Our family has been abundantly blessed. My sister attended Northeastern Bible College, and went on to work as a receptionist and team worker at Billy Graham's head office in Minneapolis for two years. She is now in Iowa, and continues to be very successful in both top management and service to the church. My younger brother Bob is highly successful in his newspaper publishing company, The Goderich Signal Star, and is past president of the Canadian National Association of Weekly Newspapers. It has been my pleasure and joy to be in full-time service for the Lord, having pastored for over twenty-five years, with a special interest and involvement in youth ministries.

Through *suffering, sickness* and *sacrifice,* God still brings us to victory. Miracles certainly were in the making when God brought our family together.

My Mother Molded Me

Miracles, of course, can only be attributed to God. How often, though, a young life feels the hand of God through the love of a mother's arms.

---

*My father, Clarence Shrier, tells of his miraculous recovery in his book, *My God Can Do Anything.* (Beaverlodge, Alberta: Horizon House, 1975.)

This is a tribute to my mother, although I know that many men, if asked, could say, "My mother molded me." The touch of a mother's hands on the life of a boy is as the touch of a master craftsman at the potter's wheel. My mother was no exception in this regard. She had the master touch to mold me for God's service. Some say our mold is cast before we are born, but I prefer to believe that God has mothers to help make that mold.

When Paul addressed Timothy he could write, "When I call to remembrance the unfeigned faith that is in thee, which dwelt first in thy grandmother Lois, and thy mother Eunice; and I am persuaded that in thee also" (II Timothy 1:5). Timothy's mold was cast by a godly mother and grandmother. In this case mothers had influenced at least two generations for God. W.M. Smith once remarked, "There is not one great American in history who was born into a home of infidelity."

For a mother to cast a mold for God and her children she must have her trust in the Lord. Many a time my mother shared Abraham Lincoln's experience — he once said, "I have been driven many times to my knees by the overwhelming conviction that I had nowhere else to go." Mothers need that kind of faith!

Respected Mother

The present generation has lost a great deal of respect for their parents, especially Mother. Proverbs 30:11 tells us, *"There is* a generation *that* curseth their father, and doth not bless their mother."

In the face of so much inappreciation for parents I want to say that my mother has always had her family's greatest respect. She has our respect mostly because of her integrity and Christ-like spirit.

Mothers who demand the greatest respect are those with a sense of spiritual obligation. We respect mother for keeping us clean, well dressed, and well mannered, but most of all, we respect her for leading us to know Jesus Christ. The heritage my mother provided will be good for this life and that which is to come. She found in her Savior the greatest treasure she could ever share with us. Money or hard work could never have brought us what Christ brought through my mother and her faith in Him.

D.L Moody had this kind of respect for his mother. At her funeral he stood by the form of his departed loved one holding in his hands the old family Bible and the worn book of devotions, and said: "It is not the custom, perhaps, for a son to take part on such an occasion, but if I can control myself I would like to say a few words." He then goes on to say with a respect that verges on reverence, *"It is a great honour to be the son of such a mother, I could not praise her enough.* In one sense she was wiser than Solomon for she knew how to bring up her children."

Words of respect and appreciation do not have to wait for such a moment as this. Respect should be shown now! Words of appreciation should be spoken today! They may help to keep mother around for a few more precious years.

My wife writes her mother at least once a week and as her mother is crowding seventy, it gives her new desires and new hope, adding a little sunlight at eventide.

"You have been a good mother to us," said a stalwart son to a dying mother, who had been thrust penniless into widowhood and who, by indescribable hardship had sent all her children to college, only to linger unappreciated among them until a stroke laid her worn-out body low. As he said these words she lifted her weary eyelids up and sadly answered, "You never said that before, John," and then passed away.

How sad it is to live with regrets! "Thanks, Mother," is easy to say.

It isn't the thing you do, dear,
It's the thing you leave undone
That gives you a bit of heartache
At the setting of the sun.

Responsible Mother

Napoleon was once asked, "What is the greatest need of France?" His answer was, "Good mothers." Good mothers without question are responsible mothers.

Mothers need to know how to pray that they might teach their children. Dr. Paul S. Rees, a great American preacher, once said, "Mother, if you are not in love with Jesus Christ, neither your love for your husband or your children can be as fine and rich and as strong as it might be. If you are not 'a praying woman', you are cheating both yourself and your family." In other words without Christ and the ability to pray a mother cannot meet her responsibilities adequately.

Tom Paine, a brilliant patriot and sour unbeliever, said, "I was an infidel before I was five years old." What did he mean? All he meant we'll never know, but we do know that in this case the responsibility of motherhood had been shirked.

Lord Byron, whose mother, in moods of anger, would call him a "lame brat," said, "My springs of life were poisoned." What was he saying? He too was saying his mother had shirked her responsibility.

Responsible mothers are praying, faith-filled, Bible-reading mothers. God-fearing mothers have given history its greatest men. Some years ago Hudson Taylor picked up a book and casually began to read. Many miles away, his mother, especially burdened with the responsibility of seeing her son saved, went to prayer. As she left her friends and was alone with God she pleaded for her son's salvation. Hour after hour passed with that mother still on her knees, until her heart was flooded with joyful assurance that her prayers were answered. That same afternoon Hudson Taylor was led to the gleaming text, "It is finished," and surrendered his life to Jesus Christ.

Yes, mothers who have accepted their responsibility seriously have molded many a mighty man.

Similarly, my mother molded me.

13

The Angry Generation

Many of today's fathers have provoked their children and, without doubt, have produced an angry generation. Someone has asked, "Why do teenagers from good homes take dope and shock their parents with sexual delinquency?"

I'll tell you why. They're angry with their parents. What causes the youth of a big city to revolt in gang wars, creating large groups with forty or fifty members in each gang? It's anger! They have been provoked to anger by delinquent fathers. If you don't think they're angry with their parents then listen to Jim, an eighteen-year-old veteran of gang life and gang wars. He was asked, "Why join a gang?"

His answer is a revelation. "For friendship, mostly," he says. "That's something the fuzz will never understand. Where else are we going to get friendship?"

"Yeah, it's for sure we aren't going to get it from our families," interjected Paul. "My old woman ruined my old man. I never want to see her again, but she keeps popping up every time I don't need her. The only thing my old man wants out of me is money."

Paul then made a final and classic reflection when he

said, "I can remember when we were kids. We used to be alone practically every night while the old man was out gambling and the old woman was out boozing with another man."

Do Paul and Jim sound as though they are angry? They surely are — angry enough to fight back through their teenage wars. One California girl of seventeen, referred to by the writer of *Tense Generation,* went to a party, drank too much, had relations with three boys and became pregnant. When asked by her mother where her diaphragm had been, she said, with tight-lipped defiance, "In my purse." She was an angry girl and this was her way of showing her displeasure.

"And, ye fathers, provoke not your children to wrath . . ." (Ephesians 6:4). Yet we have done just that. In the words of J. Edgar Hoover of the FBI we have sacrificed our children upon "the altars of indifference." We have failed to set the kind of example in church attendance, family prayers and godly living that would make them respect us. Our sinful habits of neglect have created the same type of problem that Eli the priest faced. "Now the sons of Eli *were* sons of Belial (the devil); they knew not the Lord . . . Wherefore the sin of the young men was very great before the Lord . . . Wherefore the Lord God of Israel saith . . . them that honour me I will honour, and they that despise me shall be lightly esteemed . . . I will cut off . . . thine house . . . And it shall come to pass, *that* every one that is left in thine house shall come *and* crouch . . . for a piece of silver and a morsel of bread" (I Samuel 2:12-36). They broke out in revolt of Eli's indifference and became children of the devil only to find themselves in deep trouble.

Our youth are rioting against the lack of authoritative discipline in the home. Fathers, you don't need to worry about laying down the law and reading the riot act. Young people will get over being angry at a father for stepping on them at an appropriate moment, but they'll never overcome an anger provoked by indolence and apathy. Proverbs 19:18 says, "Chasten thy son while there is hope, and let not thy soul spare for his crying." They're angry today because we have been too wishy-washy and downright spineless in our discipline. They're upset because we failed to see to it that they did the chores around the house, let them get away with poor report cards, and never made the curfew stick. The time has come for us to put a little authority behind our words. Isaiah 3:12 is altogether too true today: ". . . children are their oppressors, and women rule over them . . ." Father's place is one of authority. He is still the head of the home.

I can remember wandering home one night long after the proposed curfew to find my father sitting at the top of the stairs ready to pass judgment. *I would have been keenly disappointed if he had not been waiting for me.*

"Now no chastening for the present seemeth to be joyous, but grievous: nevertheless afterward it yieldeth the peaceable fruit of righteousness unto them which are exercised thereby" (Hebrew 12:11).

It has been well said that "regrets are poor companions." It's better to act now and save the tears of remorse in the future. Listen to the sobs of David as he realized how he had failed his son. "O my son Absalom, my son, my son Absalom! would God I had died for thee, O Absalom, my son, my son!" (II Samuel 18:33). It's far better to live for your children than to wish you could die for them. Being tough when it counts means less trouble over failures in the future.

We have an angry generation on our hands largely because fathers have failed to exert any sound spiritual influences. J. Edgar Hoover says, "The answer lies for the most part in the homes of the nation. Many of the cases coming to my attention reveal the shocking facts that parents are forgetting their God-given obligations, and more children are being sacrificed upon the altar of indifference as parents throw aside their responsibility."

"Like father like family" goes without saying. The father leads, by God's decree. He makes the home law, fixes the precedents, and creates the home atmosphere. According to I Corinthians 11:3,8,9, father is the head of the house: "But I would have you know, that the head of every man is Christ; and the head of the woman *is* the man; and the head of Christ *is* God . . . For the man is not of the woman; but the woman of the man . . . Neither was the man created for the woman; but the woman for the man."

Here are some questions a father should ask: "What kind of atmosphere am I creating? Do we have a family altar in our home? Do we attend the house of worship on a regular basis? Do we keep the sabbath day as would be pleasing to the Lord Christ? Where do we take our children on the Lord's Day — to church, to the beaches, to the golf course, to the open highways — to God or to the ways of the world?

It's inventory time! Time for all of us to re-evaluate our roles in society and find out whether or not we are provoking our children to anger. Fathers must not leave spirituality to their wives. Adam was condemned for this mistake. (See Genesis 3.)

Praying fathers are the only answer to the dilemma and delinquency of our land. Former President Eisenhower put it well in a statement to Senator Frank Carlson: "Frank, I don't think our country will ever be the country that our forefathers had planned, and God has intended for us, unless we get back to fundamental spiritual principles." One of these great fundamentals is prayer. Prayer in the home, at the family altar, and offered with one's family in the house of God.

To practice and maintain a place of family worship is to heed the positive aspect of the apostles' appeal as given to us in Ephesians. "Ye fathers, provoke not your children to wrath." Then he adds this positive instruction, "but bring them up in the nurture and admonition of the Lord."

We not only need to have time to pray with our children but time to play with them as well. We need time to get to know them and time for them to get to know us. A recent poll revealed that the average father spends a maximum of seven minutes a day with his son. We can't always be wrapped up with success, business and social life. It makes one stop and think when a child speaks up and says, "I'm tired of baby sitters." When we have disciplined ourselves in order to have time to play and to pray it will be pleasant to hear our children express themselves as the poet of years gone by.

Somehow a fellow can't express
The feelings he has had
While through the years he has walked and talked
And laughed and played with Dad.

He cannot put in words the love
The pride that swells within,
The admiration in his heart,
Whene're Dad looks at him.

Dad is the hero of his dreams,
The king upon the throne
The pattern for that ideal life
Which he would make his own.

He knows that Dad well understands
The conflicts of his breast,
And shares the problems he must face
Though often unexpressed.

The pressure of his Dad's strong hand,
The look deep in his eyes
Speaks volumes to a fellow's heart,
When cares of life arise.

And when he kneels with Dad in prayer
Before the throne of grace
The glory of the unseen world
Illumines all the place,

How could a fellow go astray
Who with his Dad has stood

Within the secret place of prayer
Before a holy God!

And this my constant prayer shall be,
That until life is done,
My conduct here shall honour him
Who proudly calls me son.

This type of omen only occurs when fathers have heeded the oft-repeated text in Proverbs 22:6, "Train up a child in the way he should go: and when he is old, he will not depart from it." If children are angry with their parents it's likely that they have felt victimized by some false philosophy of life such as; "I shall not influence the way . . . my child shall worship, think or pray . . . let him do as he is inclined." This kind of teaching does not make for a proud son such as the poet depicted for us, but it does make him angry with an irresponsible approach to fatherhood.

I wonder if you bore in mind
That others would be trying hard
To batter down your child's guard
By luring ads and presentations
And gilding vice with new sensations
If evil things you don't condemn
You'll likely lose your child to them.

Fathers should seek God's help and ask, "What have I done to my children?" They should ask themselves if they would want to live in the kind of home and atmosphere they are providing for their children. It's time for parents to do some thinking and some praying — to ask God's forgiveness and pardon! Fathers should stop "passing the buck" and hiding in the spiritual skirts of their godly wives and mothers. They should take their stand for Jesus Christ and lead the way as head of the house.

J. Edgar Hoover says, "Our experience shows that American parents are guilty of seven major 'crimes.' I call them 'crimes,' " he says, "because they lead to crime." He lists the seven as follows:

1) *Neglect:* Both parents work, and children come and go as they please.
2) *Broken Homes:* Children pay the consequences of parental irresponsibility and selfishness.
3) *Unhappy Homes:* If parents must disagree sharply, their differences should be settled outside the presence of their children.
4) *Bad Examples:* Some children are too ashamed of their parents to ever invite their school friends home with them.
5) *Lack of Discipline:* Criminals are made, not born. Each dereliction leads to another. Freedom without discipline leads to licence.
6) *Doting Parents:* Parents who alibi lawlessness harm their children. The only way to "stand up" for your child is to face the truth with that child.
7) *Outside Influences:* Making the home a place of learning as well as a place of living is more difficult today than it was a generation ago. *Parents are responsible for what comes into the home.* With today's modern inventions "bad companions" have a way of slipping in through walls of masonry and closed doors.

Here are the real enemies to our nation — the "trojan horse" that works from inside! *We need to start training programs for parents in our churches.* It was the corruption of religion in Russia and the lack of concern for the spiritual and material needs of the Russian people that helped to give birth to communism and its anti-church program.

14

Have You Tried Prayer?

Philippians 4:6 tells us to "Be careful for nothing; but in every thing by prayer and supplication with thanksgiving let your requests be made known unto God."

"Everything by prayer" the apostle declared, because he knew that prayer was the answer. Great men in every era have believed this. If men like Abraham Lincoln could give their testimony to this generation we would be impressed with their implicit faith in prayer. During the battle of Gettysburg, Lincoln listened to the reports pouring into the white house which showed that the fate of the United States hung in the balance. Others became panic stricken. They rubbed their hands and shook their heads, but Lincoln went to his room, closed the door and prayed. Later he said of this historic moment, "I told God that I had done all I could and that now the result was in his hands; that if this country was to be saved, it was because he so willed it. The burden rolled off my shoulders. My intense anxiety was relieved and in its place came a great trustfulness."

"Be anxious for nothing," we read, and Abraham Lincoln found out just how quickly anxiety flees when we take time to pray. "Oh what needless pain we bear, all because we do not carry everything to God in prayer."

How often have we been guilty of trying all our human resources before we tried prayer, in order to draw upon divine resources? We resort too often to the finite when all the time the infinite is at our disposal. Why do we not quit trusting our natural abilities and begin, through prayer, to claim the supernatural? Each of us knows how frustrating it becomes when we have to go day after day without any answer or solution to our problems. Truly, prayer holds the answers.

Abraham Lincoln revealed the source of his strength when he wrote, "I have often been driven to my knees by the overpowering realization that I had nowhere else to go. My own wisdom and that of all about me seemed insufficient to the day."

There is nowhere else to go, but usually it takes us a long time to discover this fact. So many of us are like the lady who heard the broadcast, "The Nation's Family Prayer Period," and wrote the following story.

Her husband had lost his job more than three months before. At first they hadn't worried; there had to be an answer somewhere. As the days lengthened into weeks, then into months, the situation became more and more desperate. Their meager savings had been quickly used up — then the car had gone — and finally some of the furniture. Butch, their fourteen-year-old, left for school, and Susan, who was nearly four, finished her breakfast and went into the front room to play.

The mother sat and stared at the breakfast dishes, thinking it through once more. "There's nothing else to do," she said to herself, "nothing at all."

She got up, pulled off her apron, draped it across the back of her chair; "Susan come on let's lie down for a while," she called.

Taking the youngster by the hand, she led her into the bedroom, shutting the door behind them. She put the little girl on the bed and checked all the windows to make sure they were closed. Then she knelt by the small gas heater and opened the valve, but she didn't light the burner.

Going to the side of her frightened little girl, she sat down and waited for the end to come. A noise from the kitchen interrupted her thoughts. It sounded like a man's voice. She suddenly remembered that she had not turned off the radio when her husband left for the city to look for work. What did it matter? Let it blare! In a few minutes she would not hear it . . . or worry about her problems any more.

She breathed deeply, choking on the fumes that were slowly filling the room. Then she heard it. The sound of an organ playing a song she hadn't heard for several years. The words flashed into her mind: *Sweet hour of prayer, Sweet hour of prayer, That calls me from a world of care, And bids me at my Father's throne, Make all my wants and wishes known.*

Suddenly she was praying, tears streaming down her face. "Oh God, I haven't tried prayer yet," she sobbed. "I didn't think it would do any good. Oh, dear Lord, please help me now."

In her letter this young lady told the whole story. Somehow she managed to turn off the gas and open the windows and door. Then she took her little girl out into the fresh air. Sitting on the ground, outside her back door, for the first time in many years she prayed. As the Spirit of God moved within her troubled heart, tears of relief washed away the frustration, bitterness and anxiety that had driven her to try and escape from it all.

When her husband came home that night, still with no job, she wrote, "I had supper ready and was able to give him a few encouraging words. For the very first time, before we ate, our family gave thanks to God for what we did have. If it had not been for your radio program and that wonderful song, my little daughter and I would never have sat down to supper again."

Prayer holds the answer to all of life's frustrations, anxieties and perplexities, but we must do as the Psalms encourage us to do, "Seek the Lord, and his strength: seek his face evermore" (Psalm 105:4).

Someone has well said, "You can do no more than pray before you have prayed, but you can do more than pray after you have prayed." This woman had words of cheer and encouragement with a spirit of thanksgiving for what good she received from the hand of God. What a difference prayer makes. Do things seem difficult? "Call unto me, and I will answer thee, and shew thee great and mighty things, which thou knowest not" (Jeremiah 33:3). "Plead the promise of God when you pray," said Charles H. Spurgeon. Matthew 18:19 promises ". . . That if two of you shall agree on earth as touching any thing that they shall ask, it shall be done for them of my Father which is in heaven."

How many times I have laid my hand on the Bible, quoted this verse of scripture, and claimed it in faith as a sure promise from God to me. "Touching any thing . . . it shall be done" is the promise of God. Prayer works because God works. "If ye shall ask any thing in my name, I will do *it*" (John 14:14), is His avowed commitment. The word of God further states, "And call upon me in the day of trouble: I will deliver thee, and thou shalt glorify me" (Psalm 50:15).

The young woman in our story found that suicide means retreat and defeat. You may not be contemplating taking your own life, yet many today committing moral suicide. Men and women have quit in the battle of life. Failure and frustration have driven people to drink, divorce and in some cases dope, but few of these ever tried prayer. Isaiah 65:24 says, "And it shall come to pass, that before they call, I will answer; and while they are yet speaking, I will hear." Praise God that when we decide to try prayer He will answer before we even call, then while we are speaking he will hear our faintest cry.

One might protest, "But there just seems to be no way open to me, I'm right up against a wall." Hear then what Jesus said, "Ask, and it shall be given you; seek, and ye shall find; knock, and it shall be opened unto you. For every one that asketh receiveth; and he that seeketh findeth; and to him that knocketh it shall be opened" (Matthew 7:7,8).

There it is — the promise we need to bring us to prayer. "It shall be opened." The way shall be opened, we shall find and receive, if only we will "ask," "seek," and "knock." But, someone argues, "I'm so weak and I have failed God so many times that maybe there is no answer for me." Again, listen to what the word of God has to say, "Elias was a man subject to like passions as we are, and he prayed earnestly that it might not rain: and it rained not on the earth by the space of three years and six months. And he prayed again, and the heaven gave rain, and the earth brought forth her fruit" (James 5:17,18).

It's not a matter of how good we are or how bad. It's a matter of how desperate and how earnest we are before God. We should forget our failures and weak tendencies long enough to be honest and earnest in a season of prayer, for then God shall work for us. When we pray earnestly God will then open the heavens to send showers of blessing and fruitful seasons in our lives.

On one of my many visits to New York City with Don Wilkerson, I was made aware of an unusual situation involving his brother Jerry. I later met the man and he shared his miraculous experience in answer to prayer. In his book, *Bring Your Loved Ones to Christ,* Don Wilkerson tells of a happening involving his two brothers, David and Jerry, and Pat Boone. It reads like the other side of *The Cross and the Switchblade.*

My part in this remarkable answer to prayer is related to the rally in which Pat Boone spoke, and Jerry Wilkerson found Christ. I was to be the speaker at that particular rally but circumstances had made it impossible, so Pat Boone became speaker that evening. I later discovered the dramatic results of that particular encounter. Let the Wilkerson brothers share this story with you:

Testimonies abound as the result of parents, wives, husbands, family members, and friends having prayed on behalf of unconverted loved ones. The Wilkerson family had one of their own. My brother Jerry was away from the

Lord for years. In the Army, he started drinking. Eventually, his excessive drinking caused the breakup of his marriage. For seven years he wandered far from God, leaving his wife to raise four lovely children.

Needless to say, mother, brothers, and sisters interceded before the Lord in prayer. At one point, Jerry moved to New York to find work. He began attending some of our Teen Challenge rallies. He occasionally attended a church in Queens. Our hopes began to rise. It seemed Jerry was not far from the Kingdom of God. The drinking seemed to have stopped, but suddenly he disappeared. Mother called the place where he worked and found he had gone.

On one occasion, my brother David was driving through New York City's Bowery and thought a derelict he saw was Jerry. He was not, but we knew he could have been. David began telling Jerry's story to the large crowds attending his crusade meetings. Thousands started to pray for Jerry's salvation.

During the filming of the motion picture, *The Cross and the Switchblade*, I went on location in Upper Manhatten and asked Pat Boone, who played my brother David in the film, if he would come and speak and sing at a youth rally we were conducting at the time in a church called Good Tidings Tabernacle in Manhattan. He said he would. There were only a few days before the rally and little time to advertise it.

David was scheduled to speak and I wanted to promote the fact that Pat would also be there. The best I could do was to run a one-inch advertisement in the Daily News at the cost of eighty-five dollars. (Later I was to find out that I should not have advertised Pat's appearance. He was under contract which required that notices of all such appearances had to be channeled through his agent.)

On the night of the rally Pat, Shirley, David and I met in the basement of the church and were preparing to go on the platform when David's crusade director, David Patterson, came back to join us and said, "Your brother Jerry is in the service. He's sitting in the last row." In very few words, David related the story of Jerry's alcoholism and spiritual condition to Pat and Shirley. We then began the service. I recall that during most of the time Shirley Boone had her head bowed. After she and Pat sang and he shared a testimony, I introduced my brother (David) who was to deliver the message of the evening. Just before he got up, Shirley put her hand on David's and said, "I believe this is Jerry's night."

David read a passage from the Bible and announced the topic of his message. Then he stopped and hesitated. I knew something was wrong.

This is how he retold the incident in his book, *Beyond the Cross and the Switchblade:*

I was just opening my Bible when I saw Jerry peeping around the people in front of him. I knew what I had to do.

"Folks, I'm going to ask your patience and prayers while I do something I have never done. Tonight I'm going to give an invitation to a single person." I pointed to Jerry. "It's either going to make him mad and he'll run out, or he will step this way and settle things with the Lord. 'Jerry,' I said, 'the last time we met, I said you'd come back in your own way, when you were ready. Remember? Well tonight you have come back. Jerry, I'm calling to you in the name of the Lord. Make your decision to be on His side.' " By now everyone was turning to see who I was talking to. Suddenly Jerry, disheveled and worn, jumped to his feet. . . For just the briefest moment it was impossible to tell which way he was going to go.

But then — he ran toward me. Literally ran. He threw himself to his knees and raised his hands. He shouted, "I'm a rotten sinner. Save me, Lord Jesus."

Everyone was crying now, the entire congregation, including Jerry, Pat, Shirley, Pastor Berg, Gwen, me.

I might add, our sister Ruth who was sitting in the balcony was also crying.

We had seen the fulfillment of the biblical promise. The

prayers of our family, especially mother's, were answered at the altar that night. The entire service had been arranged just for Jerry. How did he get there? As he was sitting in a bar, leafing through the Daily News, his dilated eyes caught sight of that one-inch, eight-five dollar ad. Jerry was to testify later, "I always liked Pat when I was a kid and enjoyed his music. I wanted to hear him."

Well, he heard more than Pat Boone or his brother David. He heard the voice of the Lord calling him home. The illegal advertisement was just one of the many links in the chain of events which the Holy Spirit arranged that night to bring Jerry back to Christ and to answer the prayers of a believing family.

Somebody Prayed

Somebody Prayed, And God in Heaven heard
Somebody Prayed, A sinful soul was stirred
Somebody Prayed, A soul was born again
Somebody Prayed, Their prayers were not in vain

Somebody Prayed, A restless soul found Grace
Somebody Prayed, That soul was fully blessed
Somebody Prayed, The storm became a calm
Somebody Prayed, And found God's healing Balm

Somebody Prayed, For sin and self to cease
Somebody Prayed, And found God's perfect peace
Somebody Prayed, The songs came in the night
Somebody Prayed, And Christ became their light

Somebody Prayed, For power to preach the Word
Somebody Prayed, The Spirit was outpoured
Somebody Prayed, And Showers of Blessing came
Somebody Prayed, The Church was set aflame.
"WAS IT YOU?"
— By Arthur Currie.

Whenever men have tried prayer they have found it to work when nothing else would. Elijah tried it and God sent fire out of Heaven to consume all the unbelief of a nation.

Abraham tried it and God delivered his nephew from the fiery judgment of Sodom.

Daniel tried prayer and God delivered him from the lion's den to exalt him in his service.

The dying thief tried it and his soul was delivered from hell and led to paradise.

A few people tried praying for Peter and God broke the chains that held him, led him out of prison through iron doors and set him free.

Paul and Silas tried prayer and God shook the foundations of the prison and opened all the doors to set them at Liberty.

One person has said, "The world is full of faces; blue with worry, green with envy, yellow with cowardice, black with anger and red with shame. Yet, each can be made radiantly white by the power of prayer. For no man can live wrong and pray right, and no man who prays right can live wrong."

Prayer holds the answer for each one of us if we will take time to seek the Lord. If we could only learn to put God first — put all other duties aside long enough to pray and thus let God have his way — we would find answers that would reveal the divine pattern for our lives.

Most great men have made it because they learned early that prayer was the answer. Some of them lived and died on their knees.

Some years ago a servant of David Livingstone looked into his tent and found him on his knees. He stepped back not wishing to disturb David in prayer. Some time later he went in and found him in the same posture, and stepped back again; but, after a while, he went in and touched him, and lo, the great traveller had finished his last journey, and had died in the grandest and mightest posture a man ever takes — on his knees.

How often do we take that posture? How many times do we pray? God still answers and still lifts every care.

If your home or your business, or your individual life lacks harmony and you are frustrated, then let me invite you to try prayer. Try it now, today!

"For when we are knocked off our feet it is time to get on our knees."

After a sincere season of prayer you will feel like the poet who penned these lines:

He answered prayer: so sweetly that I stand
Amid the blessing of His wondrous hand
And marvel at the miracle I see.
The favours that His love has wrought for me.

Then he adds a few lines of encouragement to others when he says:

Pray on for the impossible, and dare
Upon thy banner this brave motto bear,
My Father answers prayer.

Look To This Day
Yesterday is but a dream and
*   tomorrow is only a vision;*
But today well lived makes every
*   yesterday a dream of happiness,*
*   and every tomorrow a vision of hope.*
Look well, therefore, to this day.